The Modern Sales Playbook

how to
be a
fierce
sales
person

The Modern Sales Playbook

how to be a fierce sales person

Know Yourself.
Know Your Customer.
Win.

ilana williams
Foreword by Gentzy Franz, Ph.D.

For media inquiries, questions about bulk purchases, permission to use any of the content of this book, or speaking availability, please contact ilana@elanconsultingfirm.com.

Library of Congress CIP is on file.

ISBN 979-8-9933637-0-7 (hardcover)
ISBN 979-8-9933637-1-4 (paperback)
ISBN 979-8-9933637-2-1 (ebook)

For Orli and Ayla—
the path ahead is boundless.
May you step into its vastness,
shaping it with your brilliance, curiosity, and love.

contents

foreword

If you're reading this, you've either chosen sales, or sales has chosen you. It's likely a combination of both—in my experience the process of self-selecting into sales as a profession is driven by inherent personal attributes that demand attention, and insistently declare: *you'll be good at this.*

This is precisely why this book is so valuable. Ilana knows this about herself, and she honors that you likely know the same about you. As a result, she isn't here to waste your time. This is not a thousand-page tome filled with jargon, charts, and "academic scaffolding." Ilana, as she admits in the first few pages, is way too impatient for that. She, like her book, is practical, parsimonious, and *fiercely* committed to external success being the natural byproduct of inner knowing. She could have written a How To book for sales (because she knows how to sell). She could have written a Be a Better You book (because she has clearly done work to be the best version of herself, as you're about to find out). But she didn't. She wrote a book that allows you to be you while simultaneously achieving the results and success you want. Each page screams: the only thing standing between you and your quota is your own uniquely effective way of showing up.

This book is really a conversation with Ilana (and trust me, she is a really fun conversation). She seamlessly weaves the seasons of life with the sales cycles—wins, losses, tears, adrenaline, the whole thing—and presents the truth that emerged organically from her experiences. The wisdom in this book is pressure tested and forged from twenty-five years of cold calls, red-eye flights, multimillion-dollar deals, intense preparation, and last-minute winging it. I know Ilana—if something doesn't work, she will not waste her time. However, when something does work, she will apply it quickly and relentlessly sell the idea/approach to others. This book was born from those experiences and that enthusiasm.

All of that said, this is not a quick-fix playbook. What makes this book unusual—and powerful—is that it insists on starting with you. Not your product, not your pipeline, not your quarterly targets. You. Because if you can't see your own patterns—your impatience, your blind spots, your reactivity—then the slickest script in the world won't help you. This book teaches you how to become *unflappable*; this is the superpower most sales professionals spend their careers chasing without knowing how to name it.

Here's how to use it. Part 1 is all about you—your mindset, your habits, your blind spots, your ways of being. Don't skim this part. (You'll likely be tempted, because you want to rush ahead to the "techniques" in Part 2 so you can DO something! Don't.) Part 1 is about uncovering the unique operating system that determines your decisions and behaviors. This operating system either fuels your success or ensures sabotage. If you skip Part 1 (don't!), you won't get the upgrade you're craving, and the software will remain as is.

Part 2 gets into the sales process itself: marketing, connecting, qualifying, presenting, closing, and all the moments in between. Staying true to making this *about you*, Ilana does not provide a prescription; she builds on Part 1, trusting that you will have the tools to settle into language and behavior that feel uniquely authentic to you, and energetically gravitational to your customer. She isn't teaching you a new language, you already know how to speak. She's teaching you fluency. She is catalyzing a reality where the sharpest version of yourself can emerge, knowing that this leads to credibility; and where there is credibility, there are sales.

Some words of advice: Play with this book. Write in the margins. Really do the exercises. Reflect on where you've operated suboptimally in the past. Allow yourself to be uncomfortable with the way you've sold, up to this point. Don't take yourself too seriously as you fumble your way through the application of new approaches. Let this book challenge and stretch you. Trust the process, *your process*, because that is the only process that will truly work for you.

Also, give yourself permission to laugh along the way. One of Ilana's gifts is reminding us that joy, curiosity, and even play are not distractions from performance—they're fuel for it. The best salespeople don't just close deals; they light up rooms. This book gives clues into why this is true, and how to make it true for you (the rooms you light up in the future will thank you).

Maybe the best part of this book? It's small. Take it with you in the car or on the plane (use it as a last-minute refresher before a big meeting). Put it on your desk (we all need constant reminders). Use it the way Ilana used *The Elements of Style* (more about that in a few pages).

When you're done reading this book the first time, you'll have an idea for showing up differently in sales and in life. After the second read-through (trust me, you'll be craving seconds), you'll likely have a go-forward plan that is uniquely and distinctly *yours*.

Ilana is highly intentional and a master of her craft—much of the joy she experiences in life is because of that intentionality and mastery. That joy jumps off every page. She simply wants you to experience joy as you invite intentionality and mastery into your work.

So:

Be fierce. Have some fun. Happy selling.

—Gentzy Franz, Ph.D.

introduction

When I was eight years old, my family emigrated to the United States. One of the most valuable survival tools I had in my arsenal was a small, thin green book called *The Elements of Style* by William Strunk and E.B. White. It was my treasured manual guiding me through the maze of grammar and usage. I referred to it countless times to support me in writing reports and annotating properly. I used it all through my middle and high school years, and it's still on my bookshelf to this day.

What I loved about *The Elements of Style* is that it was concise, to the point, well-organized, and damn useful. This is exactly the vibe I am channeling with this book. I love the idea of a short, sweet, and useful reference framework to deliver what you need without the fluff.

This efficient little book is meant to have just enough of what you need to produce the conditions for success in sales. I don't have all day, and you probably don't either. So together, we will get to the meat of things without beating around the bush.

I have been in a hurry for most of my life. My mom used to call me the tornado. I would swoop in, make a mess, and then rush to the next activity.

While I still like moving quickly, I am also committed to excellence. Things don't always have to be perfect in my world, but admittedly, my standards are high, and I like to play to win.

You probably would not describe me as a patient person. And I know I am not alone in this attribute, especially among successful sales professionals and progressive leaders. While patience does have its place in the sales process—as you'll discover in this book—I often experience my lack of patience as a kind of superpower. I love to make shit happen, now. So, like most of my projects, I want this book to move quickly and I want it to be jam-packed and powerful for you.

Drawing on 25 years of a successful career in sales, I am bringing you an easy, unpretentious framework for sales and business professionals. It is an exploration of what I have experimented with and experienced while working with executives and companies. Simply put, it is what works. This framework is true in the marketplace and also in life, if you choose to apply it universally. Whether you are selling a product or service or you are a strong business professional out to make a name for yourself, this book is for you.

I am a sales professional at heart. I started my career in health-care capital equipment sales for a large global conglomerate. I loved my sales job and I have always loved salespeople. There is so much to love about this profession and those who embark on it.

The role of a sales professional is full of energy, vitality, fear, and adrenaline. Whether the stakes are small or large, a massive dopamine surge awaits. Sales professionals require a broad emotional range as they navigate the highs of huge, energizing wins, the lows of big, depressing losses, and everything in between. It's hard to lose and get back up again. And that's exactly what salespeople do. We are willing to put in the work to grow and learn, practice, and create. High risk, high reward.

Successful salespeople must be driven, passionate, and persevering to endure the risk of losing. We all lose, no matter how good we are. Successful salespeople prove their worth in the world, want to make themselves and their family proud, and want to show up as reliable and effective. They are willing to go on an adventure, learn things, win a victory with that newfound knowledge—or lose a well-fought battle—and then return home transformed.

Many salespeople are out to create a life for themselves and their family that they were not granted in their childhood. They want to take care of themselves, produce stability—financially and otherwise—and take care of those they love because fundamentally, at their core, they felt somewhat unsafe and perhaps not taken care of early in their life. This drive to protect is the fire of the sales professional, the passion of creating for themselves what their parents could not or did not do for them in their childhood. Even those who do not come from humble beginnings are often out to prove themselves in the same way. They want to show that they are good enough or better than. Strong salespeople are badasses and highly intelligent, usually witty and hilarious. They are powerful communicators, they create impressive connections, and they are courageous enough to bet on and invest in themselves. This is why I love working and playing with them (you) so much.

I am not a researcher or academic. I am not here to drown you in academic jargon or bore you with lengthy dissertations. A plethora of references already exist on what to say in certain situations or what tactic to use if a customer objects to your offer. While all of that is useful, I find what is currently available gravely lacking. Because there are so many tools and techniques to choose from, when you are in the moment with a customer, you can feel like, "Shit, what is the right thing to say now?!" or "What is the 'right' tool for this situation?" How do you know what to say in the moment to progress the deal, or to close a deal? How do you handle the current objection someone is posing?

Should you choose to embark on playing with the principles and practices in this book, you will have access to an intelligence beyond what is written here or in any other book. You will be able to tap into a wellspring of wisdom, sourcing the right words to say and the right actions to take to create the outcomes you are after. You will be "unmessable with." Even in the midst of heavy, challenging times, you will be able to draw upon a deep reservoir of intelligence, wisdom, knowledge, and way of being to create the life you want.

There are exercises and inquiries ahead in this book that will take time and reflection. The book is split into two parts. I hope you consider playing with each of the parts like a new game you are learning, as they are meant to support you in your journey of developing mastery in sales.

The first part is dedicated to an exploration of yourself, your prospective customer, and the fundamental human condition. I want you to be better acquainted with yourself so that you unveil what gets in the way of reaching your goals. If you become aware of what is stopping you, bringing any blind spot into crystal-clear focus, you will have the agency to address it. It's important to understand that this isn't about becoming a different person. It's about uncovering the best version of yourself that's been there all along, hidden beneath layers of protective mechanisms and learned behaviors. As you peel back these layers, you will find that you have an innate ability to navigate challenges, connect with others, and achieve your goals in ways you never thought possible.

So, I invite you to dive in. Embrace this journey of self-discovery and growth. It may not always be comfortable, but I promise you, it's worth it. The person you'll become—resilient, self-aware, and truly "unmessable with"—will be equipped to handle whatever life and business throw your way, creating success and fulfillment on your own terms. The point of putting in this work now is to make doing your job easy in the long term.

The second part of the book is dedicated to the sales process. You will develop clear and refined language for each part of your sales process. And it will be yours, not a canned script. In my experience, when a professional sharpens their linguistic ability, their credibility and results soar.

Thank you for trusting me. I want you to play, expand, and kick ass out there!

> *"The guide ambitious sales professionals have been waiting for: master your craft, unleash your potential."*
> —Brent Williams

PART 1

Exploring and Optimizing Your Human Condition

CHAPTER 1

Starting Out

There are two types of people in
this world: those who know they are
salespeople, and those who don't.

—Jorge Lopez

I first encountered Jorge Lopez when I was a fresh-faced 23-year-old, just starting out as a sales rep. At the time, I was by far the youngest salesperson at my company, standing out not only due to my youth, but also my gender in a male-dominated field. Some days intimidated me, other days empowered me—it all depended on the prevailing winds.

Jorge was a sales superstar. Successful, classy, and upbeat, he always treated me with kindness. He managed a key territory in South Florida and absolutely crushed it. In contrast, I was tasked with selling equipment that had not yet gained much traction in my new territory. I dove in headfirst, not realizing the uphill battle ahead. We had single-digit market share while our top competitor commanded over fifty percent with very satisfied users. Ignorance was bliss in a way—I had no clue how tough it would be to achieve our sales goals.

My initial years on the job ranked among the most challenging periods of my life. I was uprooted from New York City to Orlando with no contacts or friends in my new town, plunged into the deep end of adulthood. I picked Orlando over Tampa, figuring the airport's central location and proximity to theme parks made it more convenient. I rented an apartment well-suited for my travels by car and plane. What I failed to account for was that Orlando's two major hospital systems already had exclusive deals with my competitors, which left me with minimal leverage. To drum up new business, I had to venture outside Orlando those first few years. Most weeks I'd hit the road in my Chevy Impala on Monday, calling on accounts up and down the coasts before dragging myself home Thursday or Friday.

Spending time with colleagues provided both work opportunities and social connections. Jorge was always a bright spot. He was knowledgeable, fun, hilarious, and generous about involving me with his clients. Working with him gave me hope amidst the slog of prospecting. His customers adored him, and his intro was my ticket to getting a foot in the door. Jorge's identity and relationships were so strong that anyone he brought to a customer visit gained instant credibility.

His way of being was infectious. People, myself included, relished how he made them feel. How could you not? Well-read, articulate, honest, playful, and fiercely loyal to his tribe, if Jorge considered you part of his inner circle, you knew it and it felt amazing. He taught me that sales mastery boils down to forging genuine human connections. The natural result is a virtuous cycle of promises made and kept, and trust earned.

Jorge seldom lost business, and when he did, he quickly shook it off. At least, that was how it seemed to me. He later told me otherwise, but I would have never guessed that losing a deal got to him.

He won far more than he lost, and while undoubtedly a hard worker, he made it look effortless. The man loved his job and made each person he dealt with feel like the center of his universe. Everywhere we went, folks knew him. Janitors, receptionists, technicians, imaging technologists, directors, doctors, CEOs. Everyone. They nicknamed him "the mayor" since he knew them all. I couldn't help but grin in his presence. When he needed something, without fail people would move mountains for him, not from a sense of obligation, but from a genuine desire to take care of him the way he took care of them. Whether it was placing an order, expediting a delivery, or arranging an executive meet-and-greet, somehow he always pulled it off. Even when it was difficult, he made it seem easy, navigating the world with grace, laughter, and stellar results. Jorge showed me the immense power of building authentic relationships over time, consistently delivering on his trustworthy identity. True sales mastery isn't just about closing the deal, claiming victory, and crossing the finish line—it's about being able to dictate the timeline on your own terms. When a sales professional can progress a deal's timing, where the customer wants to help you make your targets, you know you are in the big leagues.

While it took me many years of experience and study to structure my thoughts and language around the concepts in this book—of what a person can do to hone their ability to succeed in a career in sales and leadership, because let's face it, all powerful leaders are selling themselves and their ideas—with Jorge, I knew instantly I was in the presence of a master. I could feel it in my first year on the job—that sense of admiration and awe.

Fast forward fifteen years later. After several years of work experience and studying the human condition, I had accomplished what I didn't know was possible. My territory was transformed. When I started, my product had single-digit market share and now, some areas of my territory exceeded eighty percent. We became the dominant player in my territory. Wherever we played, we won. One day, as Jorge and I were casually chatting en route to an account, I asked him, "Could you teach someone to do what you do as well as you do it? Could you explain it in words?"

After a short, pensive pause he replied (I am paraphrasing here as I don't recall his exact words), "Hmm, good question. I think what is important is to care, to listen to people, to follow through. I am interested. I read a lot. I am educated and cultured. And I like to have fun. People like me, and I like to do a good job, to take care of them, so it just works." He was mostly explaining his inner world, how he loved to learn and was inherently curious, how he enjoyed what he did and brought that joy to others.

That moment in the car is when I realized that framing the methods that create workability for a sales professional is not in the common lexicon. Most strong sales professionals and leaders can't tell you how they do what they do in a way that is understandable and useful for someone who isn't quite there yet. I knew that I could explain how leaders like Jorge did what they did in the outer world, and I could also offer some experiential learning exercises to probe one's exploration of their inner world. That moment, almost a decade ago, I started writing this book. It has been a long time coming.

Shortly after that a-ha moment, I was having dinner with Jorge's boss, Lucas. He had been recently promoted from his sales role to the regional leadership position, tasked with managing a group of account executives who were previously his peers, including Jorge. Lucas and I had worked closely together as salespeople for a few years, and he knew about my personal and professional development journey. We were good friends and had a lot of fun creating success together in our shared accounts. He was like a sponge, curious about all of the development work I was exploring. Over dinner, we started chatting about my conversations with Jorge. I asked him, "What would you do if all of the salespeople in the region were as capable as Jorge?" His eyes glimmered and his grin widened. "That would be incredible, Ilana!" *Bam.* This was the moment of lift-off. Lucas asked me to facilitate a workshop for his team. In April of 2016, I did just that.

This was the launch point to my leadership journey. I became a sales leader six months later, where I continued to practice, apply, refine, mature, and transform the material in this book to create powerful results with my teams. After twenty-three years in corporate America, in 2021, I founded my own business, Elan Consulting Firm, and have been consulting using much of this robust framework to support and catalyze success with leaders and teams across several segments, from startups to Fortune 500 companies.

This framework for understanding, exploring, and optimizing your human condition is the key to becoming a sales professional who is "unmessable with."

Strategy without tactics is the slowest route to victory,
tactics without strategy is the noise before defeat.
—Sun Tzu

Below you will find a summary of the entire framework for this book. Bookmark this page and use it as a helpful reference tool. Part 1 of this book is about knowing yourself and Part 2 is about knowing your craft. Both of these are key tasks in your journey ahead. They are your strategy and tactics.

In the following chapters we will explore each of these points in detail, so that when you come back to this page, you can quickly call to mind what you are working toward in your personal development as a successful sales professional.

PART 1: Exploring and Optimizing Your Human Condition

Know yourself—learn, explore, and optimize.

Be intentional
- ➤ BE. DO. HAVE.

Commit to self-awareness

Create structures to foster your success
- ➤ Take of care of your mind, heart, and body

PART 2: The Sales Process

Know your craft.

Become fluent in the language/content of your role
- ➤ The fundamentals of the sales process
- ➤ The specifics of your business

CHAPTER 2

Be Intentional

An intention is a truth that lives inside of you.
It's more than a conscious purpose, it's the
congruence of that purpose. It requires an alignment
of all aspects of oneself. Of conscious thoughts
and unconscious beliefs, of capabilities and
commitment, when working and not. It's a state
of living in harmonic agreement with oneself.

—Rick Rubin, from *The Creative Act*

Onboarding (or Pretending My Way into a New Role)

I spent many years of my life, especially during my teens and twenties, pretending to be interested in things that I clearly was not. I pretended to want to be a doctor, I pretended to like reading Russian literature, I pretended to have my "act together." (I still do that sometimes!) I did all of this somewhat unconsciously to fit into a framework of success. Again, having some semblance of structure or framework is necessary. We need to tether to something as we strive along our way toward "making it."

There's a bit of pretending as you start anything new before you know if you really like it, if it fits into your life. When I got my first sales job, selling highly technical equipment to hospitals—nuclear medicine gamma cameras—I didn't know anything about the technology or the medicine and illnesses involved. I didn't have a clue! And yet, my job was to be the source of technical knowledge for my local team on that equipment. I was slated to present to our customers; it was my responsibility to be the expert. Wow! What an undertaking! My intention was clear: *Be strong, be open, and learn as much as possible as soon as possible.*

I remember my new boss sent me on a trip to shadow veteran successful colleagues who had been in the role for many years. I landed in New York and shortly thereafter in Boston, doe-eyed, curious, excited, and scared shitless. I knew I was lucky to land the position, to have a well-paying job with a highly reputable German Fortune 500 company. And, while I didn't know much—I was clearly pretending to have it all under control—I knew that I was ignorant and unprepared to stand up in front of a group of clinicians and "be the expert."

On this trip, I didn't even know what questions to ask, where to start. I was supposed to fly home at the end of that week with enough knowledge to do a technical presentation in front of a group of physicians and hospital administrators the following week. The only thing that matched my fear was my enthusiasm to succeed, to overcome the hurdle of embodying the role. There was something in me that I could feel, something that led me to take step after step in the right direction, although I admit that I did not exactly know it at the time. I was, in many respects, pretending. Doing my best. Being curious and enthusiastic to learn as much as I could.

I remember being in the car with one of the colleagues who ended up becoming my mentor. I didn't know the questions to ask. He was kind and gentle. I think this is possibly the biggest hurdle when embarking on something new; discovering the "right" questions to ask. What is it that I really need to know?

We spent those days chatting in the car on the way to customer visits. He shared about the technology, the business, and whatever else he thought was relevant for me to know. He didn't know the extent to which I was ignorant. You see, most people who were in the role I was given came from a technical background, having worked in a hospital with patients. I, on the other hand, was freshly graduated from business school and had never stepped foot in a Radiology Imaging Department before I took the job with Siemens. This colleague offered to help me the next week and present to customers in my territory so that I could learn what to do and say in real time. As you can imagine, I breathed a deep sigh of relief.

I learned so much that week. My brain felt like a sponge. The best part of it, though, was that I had found a mentor. I spoke to him for hours on end for the following several months. He was my life preserver, sharing knowledge and answering questions as I learned, as well as my encourager, reminding me that I could persevere. As for the presentation he gave to my customers, I learned all the content with vigor and vitality. I feverishly took notes, studied his comments, the customers' questions, and his responses. And afterward, I took the baton and closed the deal.

My intention to learn was intense and clear. And, from that, I fostered a mentor relationship. This is a testament to the benefits of having powerful teachers and mentors, people who are willing to contribute to your development and get nothing in return. There is such beauty in someone being willing to share their wisdom with you. My mentor taught me much of what I needed to know to fumble my way through those first couple of years on the job. I honestly don't know what I would have done without his support. I am grateful, and this fueled my desire to return the favor for so many others as I matured in my career.

As I gained more knowledge and experience, about a year in, I realized that I loved what I was doing. It was scary, exhilarating, full of nuance, and intellectually stimulating. This was the first of what became several necessary pitstops of checking in with myself about my fit in my role—am I pretending to like what I am doing or is this a true fit for me? Do I know enough to make the call?

When considering what you are going to sell, what product and company you choose to represent, it is important to discern whether you actually believe in what you're saying. This is where authentic intention and results intersect. If you don't believe what you are saying, people will see right through you. Even if you think you're a great actor, people can feel it when something is off. It takes a lot to keep up appearances, and eventually, most people get tired.

I encourage you to pretend to the degree that you learn enough and then make a decision about whether you can authentically be the face of whatever it is you are positioning in the marketplace. This is where the alignment of intention and purpose presents itself and mainfests in your own experience of the day-to-day and your satisfaction. If you don't have to pretend, if you really are loving what you do, and if it aligns with your truth and your intention, then the likelihood is much higher that you will have job satisfaction and success in the marketplace.

Remember, just like I did with those nuclear medicine gamma cameras, you might start off feeling like you're in over your head. But with the right mentorship, a willingness to learn, and the courage to be honest with yourself about whether the role truly fits you, you can transform that initial pretending into genuine expertise and passion. It's a journey, and it's okay to feel uncertain at first. What matters is your commitment to learning, growth, self-awareness, and your ability to align your work with your authentic self over time.

KEY TAKEAWAYS

➤ Be strong, be open, and learn as much as possible as soon as possible.

➤ A big hurdle in embarking on something new is discovering what the right questions are.

CHAPTER 3

Your Way
of Being

As explored in the last chapter, powerful professionals are intentional. And their intentions are authentic to who they are. They adapt, learn to release what doesn't fit in their lives—that which counters their intention—and choose to mindfully expend energy toward actions that feel aligned. They are deliberate with how they allocate time and effort, and their results show it.

Powerful salespeople know what they are out to create, what they need to do, and how they need to show up in the world to make it happen. They embody a way of being that works to produce the outcome.

I introduced Jorge to you in Chapter 1 because he is a perfect example of being intentional in creating the outcomes he sought. His goals were clear and they were aligned with who he is. He was out to produce business success joyfully—close deals in a timely fashion while creating customer satisfaction—and most importantly, he was intentional in having fun doing it.

> **Disclaimer:** Jorge never claimed that the job should always be fun, enjoyable, and fully aligned—and I agree. That said,

the great majority of the time, the joy and flow was and is his embodied experience.

One of the best parts of being in a revenue-generating role is that the goals, business targets, and/or KPIs (Key Performance Indicators) are clearly defined, and are measured against your results in black and white. Of course this can also be challenging, but the absence of ambiguity regarding your performance can be a huge gift if you see it as an opportunity to fuel your learning. For salaried employees, knowing whether they are performing to an acceptable or high standard is much more likely to be ambiguous and at the mercy of their leadership's willingness to communicate. Sales professionals have clarity and transparency in their performance and don't have to wait for a formal annual review to assess whether they are satisfying their obligations. How brilliant is that!

The heart of this chapter is an exercise called *BE. DO. HAVE.* that you can put to powerful use in your life to be intentional and deliberate in creating the results you want.

I will walk you through it as a step-by-step overview and then give you specific instructions to work the exercise. Get a piece of paper and a pen, and read on!

EXERCISE

BE. DO. HAVE.

STEP 1: Think for a moment about what it is that you want to HAVE in life. Since you are reading this book, I think it's safe to assume that you want to meet or exceed your targets. Great! Put it on the list. I also encourage you to consider what you want beyond that. What do you want in life that will be fueled by your business success? Maybe it's a sleek, luxurious car, a picture-perfect house, or even to win the affection of a certain someone who you are hoping will spend their life with you.

It is natural to ponder what you want your life to look like in terms of the things you want to have. The question of what you want is not hard to answer. Even if you do not always want to admit it out loud, you, like most people, likely want to expand your knowledge, succeed professionally, and/or become more comfortable financially. Otherwise, you wouldn't have bought this book. With that in mind, write down whatever is true for you, no matter how lofty it is.

ACTION FOR STEP 1: Write down what you want to HAVE.

STEP 2: "What are the things I need to DO in order to HAVE what I want to have?"

Maybe you need a promotion to ramp up your income to afford the dream house. Or you need to close a certain deal in order to purchase the sports car. Or you need to make time to cultivate that relationship you want. Whatever the end goal is, you devise a set of tactics and strategies that will bring your desires to fruition.

⚠ PITFALL ALERT ⚠

STOP!! DO NOT MAKE A TO-DO LIST!!

The irony here is *that in order to create the outcome, we often need to BE what we think the outcome will grant us. It's a chicken and egg question.*

ACTION FOR STEP 2: Instead of a to-do list, reflect on and write down the following: "How will I feel when I get what I want (otherwise described as the feeling state I embody)?"

Example response: *I will feel freedom, joy, vibrancy, lightness, excitement.*

Okay, put a star next to Action Step 2. We will come back to it shortly.

First, we are going to explore your body's innate intelligence.

Now, notice your body sensations as you reflect on thoughts and feelings of getting what you want. Do you feel fluttering in your chest, buzzing in your limbs? For me, when I think of hitting a new milestone in my business, I smile, I can breathe more deeply into my lungs, and I feel energy rising through my whole body.

⚡ HELPFUL TIP ⚡

For those who don't tune in to their body on a regular basis, I typically describe this as the feeling you get when listening to your favorite music. Take a few minutes to play your favorite song now, close your eyes, and feel. Notice and observe your body sensations.

I get chills and sometimes the hair on my forearms stands up. The body sensation I get from listening to music that moves me is very similar to what I described above when I think of my business growing and reaching my dreams.

Body intelligence, according to Gay Hendricks, author of *The Big Leap*, refers to "our body's innate wisdom and ability to communicate important information to us."

Hendricks describes it as "a form of deep knowing that comes through physical sensations rather than just mental processes."

You have felt this wisdom in your own body in at least some, if not all, of the following ways:

➤ **Fear:** Butterflies dancing in your stomach before stepping into that make-or-break presentation, your heart racing.
➤ **Anger:** The way your jaw locks tight when frustration builds, each tooth pressing against the next. Those rigid shoulders climbing toward your ears during tense meetings. The hot surge in your chest, your pulse drumming in your ears.
➤ **Sadness:** That familiar ache behind your eyes as the tears begin to well up, threatening to spill over. The swirling in your chest, feeling as though your heart is literally breaking.
➤ **Joy:** That effervescent lightness spreading through your chest, bubbling up your throat into laughter, making your cheeks warm and your whole body feel like it could float.

Studies have affirmed the link between emotions and bodily sensations. One of the most significant scientific studies on how emotions map to physical sensations was conducted by Nummenmaa et al. (2014), published in *Proceedings of the National Academy of Sciences* (*PNAS*). The study, titled "Bodily maps of emotions," involved over 700 participants across multiple experiments.

The researchers created "bodily sensation maps" show-ing where people felt activation or deactivation during different emotional states. They found consistent patterns across different cultures:

➤ **Anger:** Intense activation in the upper body, particularly chest, arms, and face
➤ **Fear:** Strong activation in the chest area, with cooling in the legs
➤ **Happiness:** Full-body activation, with increased sensation throughout
➤ **Depression:** Decreased activity throughout the body, particularly in limbs
➤ **Anxiety:** Intense chest sensations and stomach tension

Learning to interpret and trust these bodily signals isn't just a skill—it's a transformation in how you operate. Your body becomes your most reliable consultant, offering real-time feedback.

Each emotion has a message for us. Anger: a boundary has been crossed. Fear: pay attention. Happiness: alignment or fulfillment. Sadness: release.

The key is creating space to listen. Take moments throughout your day to pause and scan your body's landscape. These quiet moments of attention allow your body's wisdom to surface, transforming fleeting sensations into meaningful guidance. Your body is always communicating— the question is whether you're taking the time to receive its messages.

ACTION FOR STEP 2: Now, reflect back to where I asked you to annotate with a star, where you described your

feeling state. Write down three or four body sensations you experience as you embody the feeling state you wrote above next to the star.

⚠ PITFALL ALERT ⚠

The problem arises when we wait until we have ticked the items off of the list of what we want *before* we grant ourselves permission to BE happy, satisfied, and content.

Maybe you want to BE happy, enthusiastic, relaxed, calm, peaceful, or joyful, but you make those qualities conditional upon having achieved certain thresholds, goals, responsibilities, or criteria.

HAVE. DO. BE. is the way many people operate in the world. I need to HAVE the (fill the blank): financial success, house, car, amount of money in the bank. So, I need to DO a series of things to reach the accomplishment and then, I will BE happy.

Remember Jorge—he always held true to BEing a kind, playful, curious, and creative person. His success was the product of his intentionality and commitment to BEing kind, playful, curious, open, and reliable. Since everything he did cascaded from his way of BEing, the outcomes resulting from his actions were inevitable.

My suggestion is simple. Get intentional and clear about your way of BEing first! Focus on who you want to BE. Embody—feel and notice your body sensations—that way of BEing and see what unfolds. Once you step into your intended way of BEing, what to DO will be clear. And then the outcomes cascade into place.

I posit that BE. DO. HAVE. is the paradigm shift that will create the intentionality that you need to not only create success, but crush it.

Once you complete the above lists, check if you are willing to commit to stepping into that way of BEing.

Before we continue with the step-by-step guide of the BE. DO. HAVE. exercise, let me tell you a story about when I made this important paradigm shift.

As a young type A, ambitious professional, I closed my first big deal at the age of 24. I remember being elated. It was such a high. I celebrated over the weekend, allowing myself a moment of joy and contentment, and then I got up on Monday morning and started focusing on the next big sale. Soon I was working 60+-hour weeks, selling large contracts to hospital administrators. Each milestone only propelled me to set the bar higher, chasing the next big thing to reach and exceed my quota. The moments of success fizzled out faster and faster. The goal post kept extending further and further down the field.

After a few years, I knew that my energy was waning. I remember days of feeling so tired, but I kept pushing for more wins even as they became almost entirely devoid of the sweetness of victory. Somewhere in the back of my mind I knew that my pace was not sustainable, that something was really off.

Then, I injured my neck in a yoga class. (I was even squeezing in time to relax and focus on health!) Later that evening, my right arm started going numb and I could barely tolerate sitting. For six weeks, I was in a state of utter misery. Even sleeping became something to dread. When I got even three hours of rest, it was a highlight. I couldn't drive, I couldn't sit, I couldn't focus. I was in a world of hurt from which there was no escape. Even as I persevered and sought rehabilitation, I knew it was time for a big shift.

My neck pain was a glaring reminder that something had to change. I could not continue overworking and forcing myself to push through to the next hurdle. I realized that my work success wasn't exclusively what I wanted to have in my life. I was not satisfied with whatever successes (mostly financial) I was generating. My injury made me stop. Literally. And I woke up to realize that I had lost sight of my intention. I got clear again. I wanted to grow, succeed, feel joy, find more play, and be fulfilled. I realized that I had fallen out of the practice of intentionality, which is forever evolving and requires periodical revisiting to test for authenticity and awareness.

This wakeup call caused me to shift the paradigm and focus on who I wanted to BE again. I could not keep up with what I was doing. My body had revolted, and because I had time and pain on my hands, I woke up. This is why tuning in to body sensation is so important. This self-inquiry work is meant to save us from tragic situations, which tend to emerge when we ignore misalignment between our intentions and what we do in life. One of the main points of self-inquiry is to be conscious enough to proactively make moves in life that are aligned with our truth. I can assure you that this is not foolproof, that all people fall into unhealthy ways of BEing and acting no matter how invested they are in their development of self-awareness. People fall into old reactive patterns, which are sometimes sneaky and can creep back in, blindsiding us. And, nonetheless, while we can't avoid all pain in life with increased self-awareness, we certainly can avert a lot of it. We have the agency to create the life we want, the career we want, the everything we want.

I wanted to be effective professionally while balancing my work and play schedule. I wanted to be a person who has time to enjoy the wins, and to be content with my success. I wanted to be ambitious, well-rested, and playful. I wasn't willing to let go of my career in the least. Rather, I wanted to shift my experience of the day-to-day, to work smarter, not harder. Sometimes, we need big, painful wakeup calls, like my injury or a primary relationship falling apart, to smack us over the head, allowing us to shift into a new way of BEing. Being more conscious and self-aware could help you avoid the need for it to get that far, for the alarm to go off before a tragedy occurs.

I reset my intention for BEing healthy to playful, joyful, rested, and balanced. I started lifting weights for the first time in my life, dancing salsa and sleeping more, consequently feeling much more joy, strength, and energy in all areas of my life, including work.

Once I had clarity about who I want to BE, what I DO is a natural derivative that leads to creating exactly what I want to HAVE in my life.

Being intentional is a choice. Rigorously holding yourself to account, maintaining your integrity to return to the choice is a constant practice. Integrity, as my teacher Jim Dethmer of the Conscious Leadership Group and co-author of the *15 Commitments of Conscious Leadership*, says, is wholeness. The more integrity you have in life, the more whole you feel, the more energy you have to allocate to those things you love and want to create. Pay attention and be unrelentingly honest with yourself as to whether your actions are aligned with your intentions.

Consider when you set an intention to prioritize health, work effectiveness, and life balance. You commit to regular exercise and quality time with friends and family. Yet under deadline pressure, you might skip workouts and family dinner. While occasionally understandable, this pattern can become a difficult-to-break habit. Soon you feel the misalignment in your body—the tension of forgoing self-care, work-life imbalance, the drain of missed exercise, the subtle ache of missed connections with loved ones. This story plays out all too often—what starts as "just this one time" becomes a steady erosion of what matters most. People wake up years later to broken marriages, estranged children, and compromised health, having chased career success at all costs. They saved the pennies of immediate deadlines while bankrupting the dollars of their most precious relationships and well-being.

For example, I know that I want to BE an open-hearted leader, a person who is catalytic in creating transformational leaders. I know I want to BE a person who supports others to wake up to their own magic and amplifies people like you to be the truest form of yourself.

That way of BEing in the world is how I have come to the place of writing this book. My DO is now to share insights and practices for developing awareness and intelligence so that you will learn about yourself in a way that supports your success in the marketplace. At the end of that process, I—and you—will HAVE the book I wish someone had given me when I first started in this business.

I hope my examples help you see how the focus on what you want to BE results in a much more enjoyable process. This is true in sales and in life!

When you can be intentional around who you want to BE during a difficult work meeting, the meeting tends to unfold with more ease.

When you face challenges, whether they be complexities with a business deal or a presentation to a new audience, you take the time to choose who you want to BE in the room. When you are open, clear, and authentic, you can show up knowing what to do. Even if things happen that you don't anticipate (which they will; after all, you are not a mind reader!), you can find a workable way to progress the sales process.

So, who do you want to BE as you read this book? Do you want to be open and curious? Do you want to be playful or do you want to be cynical? Do you want to be analytical? Do you want to be engaged?

As you work through the BE. DO. HAVE. exercise, remember that to be deliberate and honest around this topic is to create the space of possibility. Then you can BE excited for the natural, organic unfolding of what you need to DO in order to HAVE what you want.

EXERCISE

BE. DO. HAVE.

You can do this exercise in two different ways. You can use it to plan your overall life, which I recommend doing and then revisiting quarterly. You can also use it in your day-to-day operations, before a meeting or an event.

BE. DO. HAVE. for your overall life:

Find a quiet place to sit down for a few minutes and think quietly about the life you want to have. Envision your ideal state. What are your surroundings? Who is there? (And maybe more importantly, who is not there?) Now notice who (and how) you are BEing in that vision.

Now take some time to write down the answer to the following: *Who do I need to BE for this vision to come to life?*

How do you feel as you reflect on that vision? What are your body sensations?

Once you complete this writing, check if you are willing to commit to stepping into that way of BEing.

BE. DO. HAVE. for a specific moment, meeting, or event:

Look at your calendar over the upcoming week and pick one important meeting.

Sit down for a few minutes and envision how you want it to turn out. Consider the best possible outcome unfolding and allow yourself to imagine the room, the people in attendance, and how you would feel. Now write it down.

Next, ask yourself: *Who do I need to BE for this outcome to come to life?*

Again, write it down. Use those notes to be intentional about your way of BEing when you walk into the meeting.

Choosing who you want to BE is a conscious commitment to create what you want, from an authentic place where you are willing to BE true to yourself. When you are clear on your BEing, the path forward tends to become clear too.

To BE intentional is to create the space for an effortless, organic unfolding of what we need to DO in order to achieve what we want to HAVE.

I encourage you to spend time exploring what way of BEing you want to embody in your life. The rest cascades from that focal point.

KEY TAKEAWAYS

➤ Powerful professionals align intentions with actions—they choose how to spend energy in ways that match who they want to be.

➤ Success flows more naturally when you focus first on who you want to **BE**, rather than starting with what to **DO** or what to **HAVE**.

➤ Your body holds wisdom—listening to sensations like tightness, lightness, or ease reveals alignment or misalignment with your intentions.

➤ Misalignment leads to burnout and reactive patterns; presence and integrity restore balance, clarity, and energy.

CHAPTER 4

Presence Is Everything

"Know thyself." This is perhaps one of the most overstated phrases in the English language, and yet, maybe also the most ignored. To be an effective salesperson and leader, you need to develop self-awareness. The fruits of this personal development come from unveiling our blind spots. Once you see what is in your way, you have the agency to overcome it.

Seems pretty straightforward, right? Well, not always. Learning about your personality can be beautiful and humbling. We all inherit ways of being and reactive patterns in response to challenges as we grow up. These protective mechanisms, created to cope with fear, pain, or challenges, become our operating system—our "natural" or automatic reactive tendencies. They emerge in a flash as you are triggered by anything that reminds you of those past fears, pains, or challenges, creating a protective strategy that the ego builds over time.

To progress with our personal—and professional—development, we need to learn about these patterns—how we react under stress, what scares us, what excites us, what we deeply want—and reconcile the parts of us that need healing. We don't consciously connect the dots to our past until we do this work. The reactions happen so fast that they seem automatic, but this work creates the awareness and then the agency to interrupt these seemingly automatic patterns.

The outcome of this integration is the restoration of our wholeness, which fosters our vitality, creativity, and clarity on our way forward. It's about understanding and transforming our operating system, moving from unconscious reactions to conscious responses. And let me tell you, this shift is game-changing, in both life and sales.

People often ask me, "Why do this self-awareness thing? Why does it really matter in sales?"

Presence is everything. Discovering your patterns isn't just about self-improvement—it's about creating freedom from the grip these patterns have on you. This freedom is paramount in cultivating presence with a customer. Without it, we can easily get hijacked out of a conversation because we get caught up in our head about whatever insecurity is triggered.

Think about it: How many times have you been in a crucial meeting, only to find your mind wandering to thoughts of self-doubt or worry? Maybe you're presenting to a high-level executive and suddenly that voice pipes up: "You don't belong here. They're going to see right through you." Before you know it, you've missed half of what the client said because you were too busy battling your inner critic.

This is where the rubber meets the road in sales. If we're not present, we can't respond effectively. We miss subtle cues, fail to ask the right questions, and lose the opportunity to build genuine connections. Our ability to be fully present—to listen deeply, to respond authentically, to adapt in the moment—is directly tied to our level of self-awareness and our capacity to recognize and release our patterns.

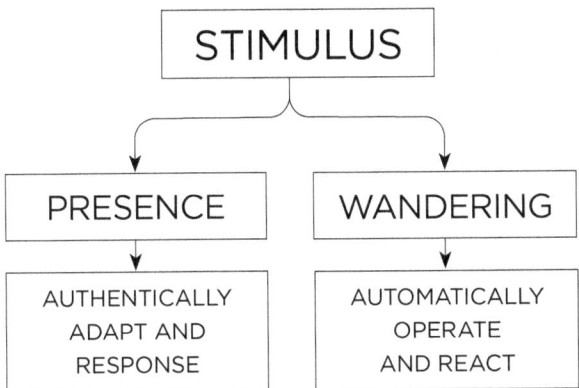

I gratefully acknowledge Dr. Gentzy Franz for his valuable contribution in creating and designing the "Stimulus-Presence-Wandering" conceptual diagram, which effectively illustrates this chapter.

KEY TAKEAWAYS

➤ Cultivating presence with a customer (and anyone else) is a skill rooted in self-awareness. It is crucial in sales because it allows you to listen attentively, adapt authentically and respond effectively.

➤ Moving from unconscious reactions to conscious responses is a game-changing shift, both in sales and in life.

CHAPTER 5

Engage Trusted Mirrors

Self-awareness requires more than just internal reflection. We need clear, unfiltered feedback from people who see us clearly and care enough to tell us the truth. These trusted mirrors in our lives—mentors, coaches, trustworthy colleagues, close friends, and certain family members—help us see our blind spots and patterns we might otherwise miss or deny.

Choose these trusted people carefully. Look for those who consistently demonstrate both courage and care: the courage to tell you difficult truths and the care to do so with your growth in mind. They are the ones who will point out when you are falling into old patterns, who will challenge your stories about yourself, who will celebrate your genuine progress while keeping you honest about your work-in-progress areas.

These relationships require mutual trust and vulnerability. You must be willing to hear hard truths without becoming defensive, and they must be willing to risk temporary discomfort for your long-term growth. When you find these trusted mirrors, cherish them. They are invaluable allies in your journey of self-discovery and growth.

The Inner Critic

The tendency to listen to and ruminate in self-doubt is one of the most common patterns that even the most successful, self-aware people experience. In psychology circles, this is often referred to as the "inner critic." The voice of the inner critic can be loud and cruel.

Some people experience the inner critic in the form of imposter syndrome. It's that nagging voice of self-doubt that just won't quit. I have felt it countless times in my career, even as I have climbed the ladder of success. It's as if there is a disconnect between what others see and what I feel inside.

Getting familiar with your inner critic, observing it, becoming its witness—but not identifying with it—can break its grip.

EXERCISE

Questioning Your Inner Critic

1. Sit quietly and reflect on the most recent situation where you experienced self-doubt, insecurity, a lack of confidence, or imposter syndrome. Write what the voice of your inner critic was telling you.
2. Consider from whom you learned or inherited this narrative. Once you isolate who bequeathed this narrative to you, contemplate how the narrative was true for the original owner's experience of life, separate from your own.

3. Find three points of evidence for how the narrative is true for him/her and not true for you.

A commitment to this work can be fun, revitalizing, wonderful, and extremely challenging and humbling. It takes time to unravel the complex web of our egoic protective mechanisms. And, it's worth it. There's a sense of freedom, liberation, agency, empowerment, and choice as we learn and grow.

There are many ways to cultivate self-awareness. Find the ones that resonate with you, such as therapy, mentoring, journaling, self-help books, developmental programs, experiential retreats, or personality assessments.

Scarcity

Much of the formation of my strong, outgoing, charismatic, and ambitious personality was the result of financial challenges my family faced when we moved to the United States. Early on, my life seemed unsafe, so I moved into action to produce safety and security. I grew up with a mother who was scared for her own survival, and her insecurity helped me foster a voracious desire to do powerful things in the business world so that I could be valuable, make money, and therefore be safe.

An exercise I did in a development course revealed much about my motivations. Here's part of my response:

"When I was eight years old, I began to notice fear about the future in my family. We had just moved from Israel to the United States, and there was frequent stress about money, which was always scarce. I recall being scared about not having enough, anticipating when the next problem would surface. I didn't feel safe. This produced a fiery ambition to have financial freedom in my life, for myself, my kids, and even my parents."

These kinds of discoveries have so much information for us. We can't intentionally create who we want to BE without knowing who we are and who we have been. The work of self-awareness is like shining a spotlight on our blind spots. When we get gripped or triggered with reactivity, we veer off course of our intention unknowingly. I often call it a tornadic swirl because it's like a gust of wind that whisks us out of presence.

Interrupting Reactivity: The Path Back to Presence

"Between stimulus and response there is a space. In that space is our power to choose our response. In our response lies our growth and our freedom."
—Viktor E. Frankl

Reactivity costs tons of energy. Self-awareness enables you to spot all the places where you're leaking energy. For most of my life, I didn't believe in myself. This may sound surprising coming from a successful business professional. My personal narrative tells of a woman who is tough, resilient, intelligent, willful, and accomplished, but the truth is that usually, it's not until I feel like my life depends on it that I'm able to push myself beyond major boundaries.

What I've learned is that when I allow myself to feel fear and accept myself for feeling what I feel in the moment, find compassion for myself and wisdom in the experience, the grip of fear loosens. When I speak it, allow it, and acknowledge it, the fear begins to dissolve. By giving attention to restoring myself and releasing shame through openness and vulnerability, I interrupt the pattern. This practice helps me conserve energy that would otherwise leak away, leaving me with more resources to achieve my goals.

Knowing yourself takes courage, humility, vulnerability, strength of character, self-trust, and a network of love. But if you find all the ways that you leak energy, you, too, can interrupt your patterns of reactivity and amplify your energy toward a focused, targeted, deliberate, and conscious goal.

So, know yourself. Use the avenues provided or find what works for you to create self-awareness. Gain a deep understanding of your core wounds. Whatever method you choose, consider it an investment in learning about yourself as a mirror for most people. Each of us has our own flavor of the inner critic. Once you know yours, you'll likely be able to be with others in a new light.

By doing the work to understand and release these patterns, we create space for true presence. Instead of being caught in a reactive loop, we can choose our response. We can stay grounded in the face of challenges, remain curious when faced with objections, and maintain our composure even when the stakes are high.

This presence is what allows us to build trust in ourselves and others in us, to truly hear and understand our customers' needs, and to offer solutions that genuinely serve them. It's what transforms a transactional interaction into a meaningful relationship. And in the world of sales, that difference is everything.

EXERCISE

Uncovering Your Reactive Patterns

1. Reflect on a recent challenging situation in your sales career. Perhaps a deal that fell through, a difficult conversation with a client, or a presentation that didn't go as planned.

2. Write down your immediate emotional reactions. Were you angry, disappointed, anxious, or something else?

3. Now, dig deeper. What thoughts were running through your mind? Write these down, uncensored. For example: "I'm not good enough," "They'll never work with me again," or "I always mess up the important stuff."

4. Consider your physical reactions. Did your heart race? Did you feel a knot in your stomach? Sweaty palms? Note these reactions.

5. Think about your behavior following this situation. Did you avoid similar situations afterward? Did you overcompensate in your next interaction? Or perhaps you beat yourself up internally?

6. Now, take a step back. Can you identify any patterns in your reactions? Do these thoughts, feelings, or behaviors show up in other areas of your life?

7. Reflect on your past. When is the earliest time you can remember having similar reactions? What was happening in your life then?

8. Finally, imagine you're observing this situation as a neutral third party. What advice would you give to yourself? How might you respond differently if you weren't caught in your habitual pattern?

By working through this exercise, you'll start to uncover your reactive patterns. Remember, awareness is the first step to change, but awareness alone isn't enough. Finding acceptance and self-compassion is necessary to forge new patterns.

Your reactivity patterns served you well for much of your life. You were smart and effective, using these patterns to protect yourself from harm, disapproval, and loss of control. These creative strategies got you this far. And yet, what got you here won't get you where you want to go. We often sense this truth most acutely when we're caught in that reactivity.

The good news is that you are powerful enough to develop new patterns. Once you recognize your current reactivity patterns, you can begin to interrupt them and choose more empowering responses.

KEY TAKEAWAYS

➤ Self-awareness isn't just inward—trusted mirrors (mentors, coaches, friends) reveal blind spots by telling you the truth with your growth in mind.

➤ The inner critic is a common form of reactivity, often showing up as self-doubt or imposter syndrome. Notice it, but don't identify with it.

➤ Reactivity drains energy. Awareness and self-compassion interrupt the cycle and restore presence.

CHAPTER 6

Tools for Interrupting Reactivity Patterns

When we are stuck in reactivity, we tend to be in a cognitive emotive loop. When we think a thought, our bodies feel sensations with emotions that arise from the thought, which triggers more thought, more body sensation, and more emotions, and on and on.

Even the most advanced, self-aware professionals go through this kind of stuck. Consider these common scenarios where intense emotions can hijack our ability to think clearly:

➤ A sales colleague arrives unprepared to an important client presentation, leaving you scrambling to cover their portion.

➤ Your boss publicly criticized your work in front of the entire team during a meeting.

➤ A client becomes hostile and starts yelling at you over the phone.

➤ You discover a teammate has been taking credit for your ideas behind your back.

➤ Technical difficulties cause your presentation to crash during a crucial pitch.

➤ The customer surprises you and tells you that the deal has gone to your competitor.

In any of these moments, there's often a spit-second thought—"oh no, this is bad"—followed by a gut-dropping feeling as fear swirls and heat rises in your cheeks. Then come thoughts like "this could ruin everything" or "I don't know what to do." Fear continues to churn, blame thoughts emerge, and anger unfolds with tense shoulders and clenched jaw.

In moments like this, the best way to shift your state—mind, body, and emotion—is through breath, movement, and sound.

⚡ HELPFUL TIP ⚡

When you feel anxiety or panic about to set in, I recommend doing four sets of box breaths. Inhale through the nose for a count of 4, hold the breath for a count of 4, exhale through the mouth for a count of 4, and hold the breath out for another count of 4. Repeat for 2 minutes.

Breathwork

When you feel activated by fear or other challenging emotions, your body floods with adrenaline, triggering the fight-flight-freeze response. This biological reaction, while protective, can hijack your ability to think clearly and respond intentionally. The good news is that you can interrupt this reactivity pattern through simple breathing exercises.

The easiest technique is 4x4 breathing: inhale for four counts and exhale for four counts through your nose, without holding the breath. This practice gives your mind a focused task (counting) while allowing your body to settle. The science behind the way this simple exercise works is compelling. Research from the *Journal of Clinical Investigation* (Cryer et al., 1980) and data from the National Library of Medicine show that epinephrine (adrenaline) has a plasma half-life of just 2–3 minutes in your bloodstream. By continuing this breathing pattern for even a few minutes, you actively support your body's natural return to baseline as stress hormones dissipate.

What makes this technique particularly powerful is its subtlety. You can practice it anywhere—even in a high-stakes boardroom meeting—without drawing attention. This combination of biological efficiency and practical accessibility makes conscious breathing my go-to strategy for interrupting reactivity patterns and regaining presence.

There are a plethora of breathwork choices beyond the ones listed here, but the ones below are my top picks.

➤ **4-7-8 Breathing.** A variation of pranayama breathing studied in clinical research, this technique has been shown to reduce anxiety and promote parasympathetic activation (Zaccaro et al., *Journal of Clinical Medicine*, 2018). Inhale through your nose for 4 counts, hold for 7, then exhale passively and completely through your mouth for 8 counts. Research at the Harvard Medical School suggests this pattern helps regulate the autonomic nervous system and reduce stress response.

➤ **Box Breathing.** This technique, studied at the University of Arizona's Department of Psychiatry, demonstrates significant effects on autonomic nervous system balance. Create a four-sided rhythm: inhale for 4 counts, hold for 4, exhale for 4, hold empty for 4. Research published in *Frontiers in Psychology* (2017) indicates this pattern helps improve cognitive performance under stress.

➤ **Diaphragmatic Breathing.** Studies at the Department of Physical Therapy at National Taiwan University show that this technique significantly impacts physiological stress markers. Place one hand on your chest and another on your belly. Inhale through your nose, directing breath to expand your belly rather than chest. *The Journal of Neurophysiology* (2018) reports this practice improves heart rate variability and reduces cortisol levels.

Movement and Expression

In-the-Moment Techniques

Wiggling or Tapping. Whether it's your foot under the table or your fingers on your leg, this subtle movement can work wonders. I know it seems minor, but don't underestimate its power. By wiggling or tapping, you're giving your body a physical outlet for any pent-up energy. Plus, it shifts your focus, even if just for a moment, from the source of your anger to the rhythm of your taps or the wiggling of your limbs. This brief redirection can be enough to interrupt the anger cycle and help you regain some composure. It's a discreet method you can use anywhere, anytime—during a tense meeting, a frustrating phone call, or even stuck in traffic. So next time you feel that familiar anger bubbling up, try a little tap-tap-tap and feel the difference.

After-the-Fact Release Techniques

When you have privacy and space to process what happened, these more intensive techniques can help you fully release stored emotional energy:

> ➤ **Physical Exercise.** Go for a run or lift weights at the gym. Any intense exercise will do. The goal is to break a sweat and break the anger's hold on you.

> ➤ **Bat a Pillow.** My highest recommendation is the anger release bat practice. Get a full-size foam bat and find a sturdy pillow or couch. Set a timer for five minutes and let loose hitting the pillow or couch with the bat. Don't stop, even when it feels awkward or uncomfortable. This is your time to release that pent-up energy. Just remember, safety first—be aware of your surroundings. After your batting session, take a moment to write in a stream of consciousness. Let your thoughts flow onto paper without editing or judging. You might be surprised at the creativity and insights that emerge—a solution to a problem you've been grappling with or a new perspective on a situation. You may even uncover how to win a deal that seems lost!

> ➤ **Journaling/Writing and Stomping.** Another expressive release practice is to write down what's angering you on a piece of paper. Then stand on it, stomping and tearing with your feet until the paper is in shreds. It's a tangible way to process your emotions.

> ➤ **Make Noise.** During these exercises, don't hesitate to make noise! I highly recommend that you yell, grunt, or growl—whatever feels natural. It might feel unusual at first, but expressing yourself vocally can be a powerful release. I invite you to match your internal state with a sound.

Remember, anger is concentrated emotional energy. By channeling it through these activities, you're not just letting off steam; you're interrupting reactive patterns and potentially unlocking creativity and new insights. Give these techniques a try next time anger visits, and see how it can transform your emotional landscape.

Quick Reference Guide

For immediate Anxiety and/or Anger Relief:

- ➤ 4x4 breathing: Inhale 4 counts, exhale 4 counts (can be done anywhere)
- ➤ Box breathing: Inhale 4, hold 4, exhale 4, hold 4 (deeper reset)
- ➤ Subtle tapping or wiggling under the table during tense moments

For Anger Processing (when you have privacy):

- ➤ Vigorous exercise: Running, weightlifting, anything that breaks a sweat
- ➤ Bat practice: 5 minutes hitting pillow with foam bat, then stream-of-consciousness writing
- ➤ Paper stomping: Write anger down, then stomp and tear the paper with your feet
- ➤ Make noise: Yell, grunt, or growl—match your internal state with sound

Remember: Anger is concentrated energy. When released properly, it often unlocks creative solutions and insights that your rational mind couldn't access while emotionally charged.

KEY TAKEAWAYS

Why Physical Release Matters

Emotions aren't just mental experiences—they're stored in your body as physical energy. When anger or anxiety gets trapped without expression, it creates tension, clouds judgment, and keeps you stuck in reactive patterns. Think of emotional energy like steam in a pressure cooker: without a release valve, the pressure builds until something gives.

The beauty of tangible release practices is that they honor the body's natural wisdom. Your nervous system doesn't distinguish between a real threat and a perceived one—whether you're facing a saber-toothed tiger or an unprepared colleague, your body floods with the same fight-or-flight chemicals. Physical movement and expression help metabolize these stress hormones and signal to your nervous system that the threat has passed.

Exploring Your Motivations

Before my leadership and sales workshops, I meet with each participant individually to explore their personal motivations. As a reader, feel free to consider yourself a participant. This exploration will help you understand what drives you, what you deeply desire, and what moves you to action. When you understand the "why" behind your goals, you can align your way of being with your deepest aspirations while pursuing external markers of success. Both matter—your internal truth and your external achievements can work together to create fulfillment.

This reflection often reveals surprising insights. Maybe you think you want that business deal because it will get you the money or the promotion, but deeper reflection shows you're really seeking a sense of impact and recognition. Or perhaps you believe you want to hit your sales targets to prove yourself, when what you truly desire is the freedom and peace of mind that financial security brings.

To encourage this self-reflection, work through the next exercise.

EXERCISE

For the sake of what, do I do what I do?

Watch the movie *The Pursuit of Happyness*. This film is based on the life of Chris Gardner (played by Will Smith), a struggling salesman who embarks on a journey full of tremendous obstacles for the sake of his son, himself, and their future. The story inspires thoughts of resilience, identity, despair, survival, perseverance, ambition, and much more.

As you watch the movie, contemplate the following two prompts:

"For the sake of what—person(s), places, things, goal(s), ambition(s), vision(s), passion(s)—do I do what I do? Who or what is my why?"

And/Or

"What constitutes my happiness?"

Next, handwrite (using pen and paper is preferred over typing) whatever comes to mind for ten minutes. My suggestion is to be unabashed, honest, and bold with your truth. There are no right answers. Consider this an invitation to craft your thinking in a stream of consciousness. This writing does not need to be edited, spellchecked, properly punctuated, or written with proper grammar. No need to spend more than ten minutes writing unless you prefer to do so.

In the last eight years, I have seen enormous benefit for those who worked through this assignment and did so wholeheartedly. The assignment is FOR YOU! It brings forth an opportunity to ponder the topic of your "why" and often brings more clarity and intentionality to how you orient your life moving forward.

As a helpful example, here is a response from a previous workshop attendant.

Lily's Response

I do what I do for the sake of my children, so that they might gain direct access to opportunities to develop their innate gifts and talents without experiencing economic insecurity or emotional abuse.

My own childhood was characterized by these two specters, and I was well into my adulthood before I was able to start to understand and unravel the sources of my anguish and dysfunction. I now sincerely appreciate that my parents—immigrants who overcame unspeakable obstacles to provide my siblings and me with a modest upbringing—did their best. They were just children when they married and the expectations of their culture and religion kept them from understanding that they could choose to separate and find love with better-suited partners.

They persevered for nearly thirty years in a chaotic and emotionally abusive relationship that imprinted each of their four children, in different ways, with the idea that love was not abundantly available, but rather something to be painstakingly earned, only to be easily lost or stolen. Similarly, they taught us through their words and actions that money was inherently scarce and that it was the privilege of a mysteriously gifted few to enjoy. We were berated for wanting things my parents could not afford and knew better than to externalize our desire for experiences that had no discernible objective other than fun. At the same time, they both instilled in me a powerful work ethic and an unshakable belief that I could accomplish anything if only I were willing to put in the effort.

It broke my heart when my first marriage failed because I had so idealized the notion of an intact nuclear family. But my sadness soon gave way to a profound determination that my children would be spared the pain of growing up believing that it is okay to tolerate abuse to preserve the veneer of unity. I found the courage to break from things that did not serve me and trust that life would work in my favor if only I were willing to listen attentively for its wisdom.

This became true not only for my intimate relationships, but also for my work. I found my voice and discovered, as I sorted through the artifacts of my childhood, that I am hardwired for optimism. I think the best of people; I expect the best of my life; and I truly mean it when I say on LinkedIn that my mission is to maximize human potential. What I don't say publicly is that I include my own potential in that sentiment, as well as that of my boys.

Having released the need to struggle and having rejected the ingrained idea that I am somehow fundamentally flawed, I now feel a deep responsibility to do all that I can to live my life well, to leave things better than I found them, to model grace and integrity, and, yes, to lend significance to the trope of the American Dream.

I do what I do so that my children, unlike me, might be

able to skip to the good part where they encounter themselves with sincere love and are able to bring their very best to the world. Nothing brings me more happiness than the thought of the two of them as fully actualized men able to discern truth from falsehood, able to courageously express who they are. And I also recognize that this sort of worldview is more accessible to those who do not have to wonder whether they will be able to afford a field trip, back-to-school clothing, or a college education. I am resolute in my desire to provide a comfortable upbringing for my children. When I scoff at the sense of entitlement that sometimes comes through in their disposition, a part of me is secretly a little proud. I like that a conscience is something I need to teach them to have and not something they are developing through the direct experience of hardship.

I do what I do to maximize human potential—starting with my very own.

—Lily Garcia Walton
Chief People Officer, General Counsel, Silverchair
June 2024

CHAPTER 7

Create the Conditions for Your Success

Let's talk about creating consistent tools and practices to keep yourself in top form. It's not just about looking good—though let's be real, that doesn't hurt in sales or in leadership—it's about feeling good. And when you feel good, you exude the kind of energy and vitality that draws people in.

Think about it: Don't you prefer being around people who have their shit together? People who look like they've got a handle on life? Yeah, me too. You want to be seen or identified that way, so what does it take to BE that person?

It comes down to self-care, supporting your vitality. When you're taking care of yourself, you're more likely to thrive. Your energy, charisma, and creativity are not magic—they're the result of good habits and self-care. If you want to crush it in sales, your self-care isn't an optional "woo-woo" idea. It's a must. If you don't feel good, you're not going to create the kind of presence and connection that's crucial in business.

Phil Stutz, psychiatrist and co-author of *The Tools*, emphasizes that our physical foundation—sleep, nutrition, and exercise—forms the bedrock of all other success. Without this base, even the most powerful psychological tools lose their effectiveness. As he notes in the Netflix documentary *Stutz*, approximately eighty-five percent of personal challenges can be addressed solely by meeting the body's basic needs.

Now, I'm not talking about some rigid, joy-sucking regimen here. I look at structuring my life—scheduling workouts, setting social media boundaries, eating well—as tools to help me reach my goals, short and long term. But here's the thing: There's a fine line between healthy structure and suffocating rules. The sweet spot for me is to have just enough freedom and just enough structure to help me flourish. For me, that looks like meditating daily, going to the gym and taking long walks. I tend to structure five out of seven days in my week. It works for me to build in freedom on the weekends. Find what works for you and stick to it. Trust yourself to know if you're creating a healthy set of habits or not. Adjust as necessary.

Think of structure and discipline as guardrails or tools. They are there to keep you on track, especially when stress levels are through the roof. They can also serve as scaffolding, practices to maintain and lean on for support when the stress is destabilizing. Usually, when I'm being good to myself and giving myself enough self-care, everything else falls into place.

Disciplined structure transforms into joyful ritual.

The magic of having a structure that works for you is that what begins as disciplined choices—to exercise, meditate, and eat well— turns into ritual because it feels so good. It might happen subtly, but the shift from discipline to ritual is a seismic one. It happens when the impetus comes intrinsically, naturally, organically, and in flow because you feel up to it, as opposed to "should-ing" yourself. When you look forward to a meditation because it will feel still and peaceful or when you are enthusiastic as you drive to the gym to meet your trainer, you are experiencing the likely outcome of designing your life to support your goals.

While I sometimes fall out of the practice of my rituals because I am human and imperfect, I know I can always rely on my discipline and structure to get back to flow.

KEY TAKEAWAYS

1. Once you commit to "knowing thyself," you're on the right path. This usually takes care of the basics of mental and emotional well-being. Proper self-care includes the physical body, the mind, the heart, and the soul.

2. Self-care for your physical body
   - Eat real, nutritious food.
   - Get 7–8 hours of sleep per night.
   - Move your body regularly. (I highly recommend resistance training 2 times per week and long walks.)

3. Self-care for your heart and soul
   - Meditate for 10 minutes a day. (Trust me, this is a game-changer.)
   - Make time for play and laughter. (All work and no play does not make for a joyful existence!)

4. Self-care for your mind
   - Stay curious and explore what interests you.
   - Find someone who can guide you—a therapist, coach, or mentor.

5. Remember, this isn't about perfection. It's about creating a lifestyle that supports your success. When you take care of yourself, you are better equipped to take care of business. Start building those habits today.

PART 2

The Sales Process

Be prepared. In other words, know your shit! Become fluent in the language of your sales process. Learn enough about the specifics so that you trust yourself and so that your customers trust you.

The following section offers a description of the sales process, as well as exercises to help you to be fully prepared. Now that you are more aware of yourself and some of the fundamentals of the human condition that are applicable to you, your colleagues, and your customers, you are ready to dive into the meat of the sales process.

Here we go! Have fun!

CHAPTER 8

Marketing

Marketing is the first step in the sales process. It's the part of the process that happens before a sales professional enters the conversation with the customer.

Marketing is defined in countless ways. *The Oxford English Dictionary* defines it as "the action or business of promoting and selling products or services, including market research and advertising." Here are a couple more definitions or interpretations of marketing:

> *Marketing is the process of getting people interested in your company's product or service. This happens through market research, analysis, and understanding your ideal customer's interests. Marketing pertains to all aspects of a business, including product development, distribution methods, sales, and advertising.*
> —Caroline Forsey, Hubspot

> *Some people would tell you that the purpose of marketing is to get your name out in the marketplace, and others will*

tell you marketing builds your brand name. A common
response is that marketing assists in generating leads that are
then passed over to the sales team and then others will say
marketing generates sales. Then there are people that will say
that marketing builds brand awareness.
—Nishan Singh, Analytico

Marketing sets the stage for your sales conversations. It's like the opening act of a play—it sets the tone, introduces the main themes, and prepares the audience (in this case, your potential customers) for what is to come. As a salesperson, your job is to pick up where marketing leaves off, building on that foundation to create meaningful connections and drive results.

The most important part for a sales professional to know about marketing is what your customer believes about you from the marketing that has happened thus far. What is the brand identity from the customer's point of view? If the customer encountered a sales professional from the company you are representing, what was his/her opinion of that relationship and sales professional? This is the context you are walking into.

Think about it. As a salesperson, you are walking into the room about to engage in a prospecting conversation—this is where you enter the sales process—and you want to be as prepared as possible.

Knowing what the customer thinks of you and the company you represent has always been a wise move in my experience. When I was selling a challenging product with single-digit market share, understanding our marketing efforts and brand perception was crucial. It helped me anticipate objections, highlight our unique value propositions, and bridge the gap between customer perceptions and the reality of our offering. This knowledge gave me an edge, allowing me to tailor my approach and address any preconceptions right from the start.

So before you step into that room or pick up that phone, take a moment to consider:

➤ What story has your marketing told?

➤ What expectations has it set?

➤ How can you align your approach with these messages while also bringing your unique value to the conversation?

By thoughtfully answering these questions, you'll be better equipped to navigate the sales process and create the outcomes you're after.

The Power of Market Self-Awareness: A Story of Authenticity and Connection

I met Michael at a personal development workshop where we quickly discovered a shared love of candid, conscious relationships—the kind where people show up close, connected, revealed, and authentic. Our friendship deepened over countless conversations about life, business, and our mutual appreciation for great food, smart people who love to laugh, and the joy of exploring new ideas together. When he shared this story with me, I knew it perfectly captured the power of bringing that same authenticity into professional relationships.

Sometimes life hands you your biggest opportunity right when everything else seems to be falling apart. For Michael, 2015 was that moment. His personal life was unraveling as he faced divorce, and he stood at a crossroads that would define not just his career, but who he was as a person.

"I had a decision to make," Michael shared with me. "Do I crumble, or do I reorganize myself and get to it?" The "it" in question wasn't just any deal—it was the opportunity to represent the sale of an iconic Nike store on Michigan Avenue in Chicago, a transaction nearly four times larger than anything he'd handled before.

Before even stepping into the room, Michael knew exactly what he was walking into. The market's perception was crystal clear: His team wasn't the obvious choice for a deal of this magnitude. The other firms bidding for this deal were the trophy players, with several high-profile transactions under their belt.

"There was a way that I could have beat myself up across all facets of life," he reflected. But something about this opportunity energized him. While his team didn't have the same trophy deal experience as some of the other firms, they brought something different to the table—a fresh perspective and unwavering commitment to excellence.

Instead of letting his circumstances get the best of him, Michael channeled his energy into determination. "I want to get this right," he decided. He pushed forward, embracing rather than hiding from his team's position in the market.

Most firms would have tried to compensate for their perceived market position, attempting to match the established players' gravitas. But Michael took a different approach. With just two weeks to prepare, he and his team leaned into who they really were—the hungry go-getters who would work harder than anyone else to make this deal successful.

The property had been managed by a large Wall Street investment bank and had performed remarkably well over the years. Walking into those first meetings, Michael knew they weren't seen as the obvious choice. But sometimes, he realized, not being the obvious choice could be an advantage.

Enter Jeff, the asset manager from the bank. With his tough New York exterior and straight-shooter demeanor, Jeff wasn't your typical investment banker. "He was brilliant in his intuition and judgment,"

Michael told me, his eyes lighting up. "Some would call it street smarts. He reads a room and reads people very quickly."

What developed between Michael and Jeff was something neither of them expected. Rather than trying to paper over his team's relative inexperience with deals of this size, Michael was upfront about it. "We'll work harder than anyone else to make this successful."

The tipping point came during those early conversations. "There was this moment where Jeff basically said, 'Yo, we're in this together. We've got to be in lockstep,'" Michael recalled. That shift changed everything. While other firms were resting on their reputations, Michael and his team "had everything to gain . . . we had every reason to want it to be great."

Jeff, with his sharp intuition, saw something in this transparency. As the process unfolded, their working relationship naturally deepened into friendship. "By the time we were ready to hit the market, he felt like a confidant, trusted advisor, and friend," Michael shared. "You're talking to somebody every day or every other day for four months, and both of your professional futures hang in the balance. We had each other's backs."

The result? A record-breaking $295 million sale (as reported in Crain's Chicago Business journal, November 18, 2015) that exceeded everyone's expectations. But more importantly, it marked the beginning of a friendship that continues nearly a decade later. What started as a high-stakes business relationship evolved into something more meaningful—a genuine connection that transcended the transaction.

This story illuminates a powerful truth about sales: Understanding how you're perceived in the marketplace isn't about changing that perception—it's about knowing how to work with it authentically. Michael walked into those meetings fully aware that his team wasn't seen as the obvious choice, but instead of trying to hide from that reality, he embraced it.

For Michael, this deal wasn't just about the numbers. It was about understanding that sometimes the most powerful thing you can do is acknowledge exactly where you stand in the market and turn that into your strength. As he put it, this deal remains "quite different than most of the transactions I've handled. Really special." That specialness comes not just from the size of the deal, but from the personal growth it represented and the lasting friendship it created.

In the end, Michael's story teaches us that success in sales often comes from having the courage to see yourself as the market sees you, and then finding a way to make that work in your favor. It's about walking into the room with complete awareness of who you are—and who you're not—and letting that authenticity become your strength.

EXERCISE

Your Brand and Your Customer

> ➤ Take a step back and reflect on the brand identity of your brand, company, product and yourself. Describe it in written form.
> ➤ What do you think your customer knows about your brand? your product? your team or yourself?— before you engage with him/her?
> ➤ Do you have a story about your customer's marketing/brand identity? What is their marketing or brand message?

KEY TAKEAWAYS

1. Marketing's Role in Sales
   - ➤ Marketing precedes direct sales engagement and sets the foundation for all sales conversations.
   - ➤ It's the first step in the sales process, happening before sales professionals enter the conversation.
   - ➤ Marketing functions as the "opening act" that sets expectations and themes for customer interactions.

2. Core Marketing Definition
   - ➤ Fundamentally about promoting and selling products/services.
   - ➤ Encompasses market research, analysis, advertising, and understanding customer interests.
   - ➤ Extends across multiple business aspects: product development, distribution, sales, and advertising.

3. Critical Knowledge for Sales Professionals
   - ➤ Understanding the customer's perception of your brand from previous marketing efforts.
   - ➤ Awareness of existing brand identity from the customer's perspective.
   - ➤ Knowledge of any previous sales relationships or interactions with your company.

4. Strategic Importance
   - ➤ Helps anticipate potential objections.
   - ➤ Enables sales professionals to highlight relevant value propositions.
   - ➤ Allows for bridging gaps between customer perceptions and product reality.
   - ➤ Facilitates tailored approaches based on existing market positioning.

5. Practical Application
   - ➤ Sales professionals should research and understand marketing messages before customer engagement.
   - ➤ It's important to align your sales approach with existing marketing narratives.
   - ➤ You need to consider how marketing has shaped customer expectations.

6. Reflection Points (From Exercise)
   - ➤ Evaluate current brand identity (company, product, personal).
   - ➤ Assess customer's existing knowledge of your brand/product.
   - ➤ Consider customer's own marketing/brand message for context.

CHAPTER 9

Connecting

In the fast-paced world of sales, it's easy to get caught up in the rush to close deals and meet quotas. But the most successful salespeople understand that true success is built on a foundation of trust and authentic connection. Before you can even begin to pitch your product or service, you must first create a space of openness and rapport with your potential customer.

This starts with being genuinely curious about the person in front of you. So often, we enter sales conversations with preconceived notions and stories about who our customer is and what they need. We might assume that they are too busy to talk, that they are loyal to a competitor, or that they are just not interested in what we have to offer.

But these stories are just that—stories. They're projections based on our own fears and limiting beliefs. To create a real connection, we have to be willing to set aside our assumptions and meet the customer where they are, with fresh eyes and an open mind.

This doesn't mean being naive or ignoring reality. It means consciously choosing to create a new story—one of possibility, partnership, and mutual value creation. When we approach our customers with this mindset, we create the conditions for authentic dialogue and discovery.

Of course, being open and curious isn't enough on its own. We also have to be authentic in our interactions. This means showing up as our true selves, warts and all. It means being honest about what we know and what we don't know, about what our product can and can't do. It also means resisting the temptation to gossip or speak negatively about competitors, even if the customer invites us to do so. To gossip is to be human.

According to historian Yuval Noah Harari in his book *Sapiens*, "The new linguistic skills that modern Sapiens acquired about seventy millennia ago enabled them to gossip for hours on end. Reliable information about who could be trusted meant that small bands expand into larger bands, and Sapiens could develop tighter and more sophisticated types of cooperation."

Be mindful to notice an inclination to gossip about a client, especially those whom you don't like, who may have done something that triggered you into reactivity. Gossip can feel like a quick way to build camaraderie, but in reality, it undermines the integrity of any relationship. It creates a dynamic of "us versus them" rather than focusing on the customer's needs and how we can best serve them. If we do slip into gossip, it's important to catch ourselves and work to restore trust and wholeness to the conversation.

Finding Compassion: A Story of Transformation

Let me share a powerful story from Kait, a mentee and a powerhouse sales professional, who transformed a challenging key relationship in her account. When Kait first encountered Sarah (name changed), several team members had identified her as a potential threat to their success. She had a reputation for being difficult, and the relationship was strained to say the least.

Initially, Kait found herself caught in a pattern of negativity and gossip about Sarah, viewing her through the lens of others' perceptions rather than forming her own relationship. This went on for many years, with Kait admitting that she never made an effort to have a relationship with Sarah: "I always just perceived her as how I was told she was, instead of finding out on my own."

The transformation began during a team exercise exploring difficult customer relationships. When asked to shift perspective and find compassion for challenging customers, Kait had a breakthrough. She began to see Sarah's situation differently: here was someone in her late sixties, still working while her husband had retired, perhaps feeling left behind or still trying to prove something to herself or others.

"She's still searching for something that she hasn't found yet," Kait realized. This shift in perspective—from judgment to compassion—changed everything. Though Kait didn't consciously change her actions, her way of being transformed. She began looking for "glimmers"—positive aspects of Sarah's personality and their shared projects—rather than focusing on problems.

The results were remarkable. In their next interactions, whether face-to-face or on virtual calls, Sarah was "sweet as pie." The relationship that had once been characterized by tension and avoidance transformed into a productive partnership. Kait reflected later, "She is totally neutralized."

This transformation highlights a crucial lesson in sales and relationship building: Often, the key to changing a difficult relationship isn't in changing your actions, but in shifting your perspective and finding compassion for the other person. When you can step out of judgment and into understanding, seeing situations from others' points of view, remarkable transformations become possible.

As Kait realized, sometimes what appears as difficult behavior might simply be a response to feeling overlooked or undervalued. "Imagine if you were an executive and there's someone running in all the same circles, but not investing in your relationship," she reflected. "Maybe she was a little annoyed that I hadn't given her the respect she probably felt she deserved."

This story reminds us that in sales, as in life, our preconceptions often create self-fulfilling prophecies. When we're willing to set aside our judgments and approach relationships with fresh eyes and genuine compassion, we often discover that the "difficult" person isn't so difficult after all.

Another key aspect of authentic connection is being fully present. This means giving the customer our undivided attention, listening deeply to their words and the meaning behind them. It means treating every interaction as important, regardless of the person's title or perceived influence.

You never know who might end up being a key decision-maker down the line. The junior associate you hit it off with today could be the CEO in five years. By making a genuine effort to connect with everyone we encounter, we build a network of trust and goodwill that can pay dividends in unexpected ways.

Presence also means being patient and not rushing the conversation. It's tempting to want to jump straight into our pitch, especially if we're feeling pressure to hit our numbers. But if we haven't taken the time to build rapport and understand the customer's context, our message is likely to fall flat.

Think of it like building a house. You wouldn't start with the roof and walls before laying a solid foundation. In the same way, authentic connection is the bedrock on which the rest of the sales process is built. Skipping this crucial step is like building a house on sand—it might look okay for a little while, but it won't stand up to the test of time.

So how do we lay that foundation? It starts with how we introduce ourselves.

Consider this inquiry: How do you introduce yourself? What do you want people to know about you? Anything? Nothing? What mood are you in as you introduce yourself? What are you trying to create from your introduction?

When I ask this series of questions to my clients, colleagues, and employees, I often get a baffled look or blank stare. Most people don't know the answer to the above questions. They often respond with their name, their role or title, and maybe how long they have worked at their company. In a large boardroom setting, where everyone isn't already acquainted, the start of the meeting is almost always everyone going around and listing off their name and title.

Perhaps your name and title is interesting for some, but most often I find this kind of introduction does not tend to create much connection. Besides the occasional benefit of lending clarity to the power dynamic in the room, very little relevant information is gained from an introduction that includes only names and titles, especially since company-specific jargon is often used for roles and titles.

Your introduction is an opportunity to create a relationship. It's an entrance point, the doorway to connection. I highly recommend you dive into this inquiry. It's a Jedi move.

Rather than launching into a canned elevator pitch, we can take a moment to share a bit about who we are as a person. What inspired us to get into this field? What do we love about what we do? What common ground might we have with the customer?

EXERCISE

Introducing Yourself Powerfully

Your introduction is a mega opportunity to set the stage for the rest of the sales process. Whenever you engage with a customer, you have an opportunity to create an identity with them, which will cascade to their willingness to listen, a key component of the prospect criteria. Take the time to establish what you are trying to create in your introduction. It is an enormous opportunity to connect, start building rapport, and gain credibility.

STEP 1: Get Present and Set Your Intention

Before crafting your introduction, take four 4x4 breaths as described in Chapter 6. Then reflect on these foundational questions:

> ➤ What is your intention? In other words, what do you want to create from your introduction?
> ➤ What do you want the person(s) to whom you are introducing yourself to know and remember about you?
> ➤ How do you want to relate to that person or the group? Do you want to create rapport, even foster a possible friendship, or do you want to skip to the content of the conversation?
> ➤ Check your internal state. It's okay if you just want to get to work, but notice: Are you feeling pressured, anxious, or rushed versus feeling open, curious, and in flow? Remember, when you're in a stressed or pressured state, it's hard to be creative.

STEP 2: Craft Your Introduction with Purpose

Write down your intended outcome—what you are trying to create—from your introduction.

Imagine you are sitting in a boardroom with a long table and 20 chairs. This is not an unusual sight in the corporate world. Most of the time, there is a round of introductions.

People remember very little, so focus on what exactly you want them to remember about you and more importantly, what you want them to feel, which they are more likely to remember. Be intentional about the feeling you want to create, both for yourself and for the person who is meeting you.

STEP 3: Practice and Refine

1. Take a few minutes to craft your introduction.
2. Stand in front of a mirror and say it out loud.
3. Assess whether you have delivered on your intended outcome.
4. Repeat steps 2 and 3 with a fellow colleague you trust to get feedback.

Example Introductions

Here are a few example introductions that weave together key elements creating emotional resonance while maintaining professionalism. I admit that there are times that traditional, straightforward introductions seem fitting and efficient such as, "Hi, my name is Ilana. I'm excited to be here. I'm the Siemens Area Vice President in the Southeast for Services Sales"; however, they miss the opportunity to create connection and context with those around you. The following are introductions with a narrative arc that connects past history, present connection, and future engagement:

Hi, my name is Ilana Williams. I am responsible for the Services Sales business for the Southeast US. I have been a big fan of this organization for a long time, having worked with you for well over a decade. Lots of the people in this room know me well and you have a very special place in my heart and I'm really excited to have this dialogue today. Looking forward to learning from you, to contributing whatever I can in the conversation, and to growing and developing our relationship further.

Hi everyone, I'm Marcus. I've had the privilege of watching this organization evolve over the past 15 years while leading our West Coast operations. Many of you have become not just colleagues but trusted friends, and I've seen firsthand how our shared commitment to sustainability has transformed the industry. I'm energized every time I get to work with this team, and I'm looking forward to diving into today's discussion about where we're headed next.

Good morning, everyone, I'm David. Leading the technology integration team at this company has given me the unique opportunity to work alongside your incredible talent for nearly a decade. I've seen your commitment to pushing boundaries firsthand, and it's been remarkable to watch your ideas transform into industry-leading solutions. Many faces in this room bring back memories of challenging projects we've tackled together, and I'm looking forward to adding another chapter to our story today.

The Deeper Purpose

At the end of the day, authentic connection is about showing up fully, setting aside our agendas, and being genuinely interested in the person in front of us. It's about creating a story of possibility and partnership, and being the kind of person we'd want to do business with ourselves.

When we approach our sales conversations with this spirit of openness, curiosity, and care, we create the conditions for trust, loyalty, and long-term success. We stop being just another salesperson and start being a trusted advisor and valued partner.

So before your next sales interaction, take a moment to check in with yourself. What stories are you telling about this customer? How can you set those aside and show up with fresh eyes? How can you bring more of your authentic self to the conversation? And how can you create a space of real human connection?

By leading with our humanity, we invite the customer to do the same. We create a space of warmth and authenticity that allows for real conversation and connection. And if we sense that the customer is not in a space to engage fully—if they seem distracted, rushed, or closed off—we have the courage to acknowledge that and suggest reconnecting at a better time.

By committing to these practices, you'll not only improve your sales outcomes, but you'll also find more meaning and fulfillment in your work. You'll build relationships that last long after the initial deal is done. And you'll discover that the art of authentic connection is the true heart of sales success.

Thomas's Story

This is a story about partnership, learning how to be an effective team member, collaborator, and trusted implementor.

I was in my role as a sales specialist for one of our product lines for a decade covering a large geographical area. I worked with many account executives who had a much smaller account list and were supposed to know everything and everyone at the account. When I met Thomas, our newest account executive, he was a few months into his role, relatively new to the team, and inexperienced in the healthcare business; regardless, I could immediately tell he had a lot of potential. My initial impression was that Thomas was a hard worker, willing to pull up his sleeves and pound the pavement. He was articulate, kind, and moderately anxious. All of his accounts were in strategic alliances with competitors so it was his job to turn customers from the competition to Siemens. I knew it was a hard job. I respected him and I didn't envy him. I had compassion for him.

Early on in his role, we worked on a small deal together and encountered a difficult loss. That year, every deal seemed significant, no matter its size. The market was dry and I was pregnant. I'll never forget how it felt to walk into this account to find out that the deal was lost, and that Thomas didn't know about it. I remember leaving the hospital and going to a gas station and calling him to share the news. I was disappointed and angry, and he could tell. When he tells the story, he describes the gut drop and fear from how angry I was. Truth be told, it was the launch point of what became one of the most impressive sales partnerships in both of our careers. This loss was our ignition switch.

We launched into action, met a few times to explore his account list, inquired what each of us knew and where our gaps were. This connection point and deep work was fun and energizing. We used the time to learn about each other and how we could help one another to create a vision for exploring new possibilities. In the process, we became good friends.

Thomas was curious about what he could say to his customers that would trigger their interest. He wanted to know what questions to ask to create curiosity, to entice a prospect with something special, distinct, and unique that could help them operationally, clinically, or both. I taught him everything I could about what made our equipment special, and shared how other real-life customers saw value. One customer increased their throughput by thirty percent by using our new products. This increased their revenue stream and decreased their backlogs substantially.

Thomas was fully on board, prepared with questions and narratives. We were out to shake it up. We produced a new awareness for new possibilities and the gaps we could work together to fill in the marketplace, while simultaneously creating connection and collaboration.

One afternoon shortly after these exploratory meetings, Thomas called me to say that he had arranged an opportunity for us to present at a luncheon with a large complex account. It would be a tough nut to crack as the people at the account had a long and very strong relationship with our main competitor. Thomas had been investing in building relationships at this account, was making headway in other modalities, and this created an opening for us to work together. I was super excited and a bit scared. I knew that the relationships with my competitor were strong and that the department manager had even worked for the competitor a few years prior.

As I walked in, Thomas told me that he was just informed by the Radiology manager that this was a "silly hill to try to climb. They don't have any plans for new equipment for this department and there is no budget available." I was unfazed. I could feel it in my gut that magic was about to unfold.

I went into that lunch presentation in such a great mood, beaming with enthusiasm, ready to connect, prospect, perform, and, dare I say, seduce. Selling is an art and a science. The art of seduction when you meet someone new and create new possibilities is one of the coolest parts of being in this role. I love presenting and they could feel my infectious energy.

After rave reviews from the presentation, where I planted a few seeds about new technology and left a lot of questions unanswered (as one should always do during a prospecting conversation), the physician, who was very highly regarded and wielded a lot of power in the organization, was intrigued and curious. The technologists followed his lead.

We moved into the qualifying phase of the sales process shortly thereafter. As Paulo Coelho says, "The universe conspires to give you what you want." From left field, we got the call that they found the money and the space to build a new department in a new tower project that was already underway. They realized that this technology would create new revenue streams and enhanced clinical outcomes. We were in.

Over a couple of months, we had several qualifying meetings to iron out the details of the equipment that would best serve them, and then it was time to close the deal. Thomas and I arrived mid-morning to meet with the vice president of Radiology at the hospital. I had a massive binder in my hands with quotes for four new systems that we would turn in to the new department on the same week that they would turn off their existing units in another part of the hospital. I had created a thorough and elaborate plan to phase and implement this new department with white glove service.

When we walked in to close the deal, I noticed that the vice president had an angry look in his eye. Gut drop! Thomas had been working with him on several other projects and that morning, unbeknownst to us, the entire executive team walked into the building noticing a very expensive magnetic resonance imaging (MRI) scanner sitting outside their entrance doorway covered in a blue tarp to shield it from the rain. This was the first piece of equipment that the hospital had purchased from us in many years. A huge multimillion-dollar investment had been left outside with a tarp in a subtropical climate.

Understandably, his boss and other top executives were surprised to see such a sight as they entered the building, and he had to answer for it. He was angry, defensive toward us, and I speculate that he felt responsible and ashamed. It was a project that he led for the hospital and everyone knew it. He blamed us for being incompetent in our delivery and rightfully so. I wanted to crawl into a hole, my heart beating fast, blood rushing to my face. Thomas and I kept quiet. Thomas's demeanor seemed stoic and unfazed. He was calm and patient, waiting for the customer to finish his rant. I didn't know what to do with that kind of anger at the time. I had yet to encounter a customer as aggravated as he was. As soon as the customer was done yelling, Thomas took responsibility. He quietly and gently asked if the vice president had anything else to say about the MRI scanner. Then he said, "We came here today to discuss the nuclear medicine quotes and to answer any questions on that project, and we would be happy to come back at another time. Would you like to reschedule?" The customer took a deep breath—I don't think I breathed until he took that deep breath—and said, nope, let's do it, I am done talking about the MRI. It took me a moment to relax. He was already there, totally present and ready to proceed. I couldn't believe it. All he needed was a chance to vent his anger and frustration, and then he was ready for our meeting. We talked about the quotes, we dotted the i's and crossed the t's, and the deal was done.

A few weeks later, in August, I was much more pregnant and we got the purchase order just in time before the end of the fiscal year. It was an epic deal, unbudgeted, unplanned for, and the biggest dollar volume business I had booked to date in my career. It speaks to teamwork, to staying open and curious with colleagues and customers, to inventing new possibilities, to being patient, and allowing people to be people.

KEY TAKEAWAYS

1. Authentic Connection
   - ➤ Sales success is built on a foundation of trust and authentic connection.
   - ➤ Create a space of openness and rapport before pitching.
   - ➤ Being genuine and present is essential for meaningful relationships.

2. Managing Stories and Assumptions
   - ➤ Notice the stories and preconceived notions you carry about customers.
   - ➤ Set aside assumptions and meet customers with fresh eyes.
   - ➤ Choose to create new stories of possibility and partnership.
   - ➤ Approach each interaction with an open mind.

3. Being Present
   - ➤ Give customers undivided attention.
   - ➤ Listen deeply to words and meaning.
   - ➤ Treat every interaction as important.
   - ➤ Be patient, don't rush to pitch.
   - ➤ Show up fully in conversations.

4. Power of Introductions
   - ➤ Be intentional about what you want to create from your introduction.
   - ➤ Your introduction is "an entrance point, the doorway to connection."
   - ➤ Move beyond just sharing name, role, and title.
   - ➤ Create an opportunity for relationship building.

➤ Consider what you want others to know and remember about you.

➤ Be intentional about what you want to create from your introduction.

5. Professional Integrity

➤ Resist the temptation to gossip.

➤ Show up as your true self, "warts and all."

➤ Be honest about what you know and don't know.

➤ Focus on serving customer needs.

➤ Maintain the integrity of relationships.

6. Building Trust

➤ Lead with humanity to invite customers to do the same.

➤ Create a space of warmth and authenticity.

➤ Focus on becoming a trusted advisor and valued partner.

➤ Build relationships that last beyond the initial deal.

➤ Discover that authentic connection is "the true heart of sales success."

CHAPTER 10

Prospecting

In this chapter, we explore the art of prospecting and the importance of maintaining curiosity in the early stages of the sales process.

The purpose of a prospecting conversation is to explore potential sales opportunities, to continue to build rapport. The outcome from a powerful prospecting conversation is simple and singular, to set up a qualifying meeting as powerfully as you can.

The biggest open flank here is DO NOT sell prematurely. "Danger, danger. Don't do it." There's no rush. You don't have enough information yet.

You need to assess whether you have a viable prospect. You want to explore whether the customer has the following: authority, need, urgency, funds, and a willingness to listen to you. Perhaps you have multiple prospects and multiple layers of prospecting that you will need to do within the account. Don't fret. This is normal, especially in complex deals, businesses, and markets.

> **Side note:** The acronym BANT is often used when discussing the criteria for a prospect. Budget, Authority, Need,

Time. I don't mind the use of this acronym, but I don't entirely agree with the B. Budgets are stories. They aren't set in stone. While funds are necessary for a transaction, budgets are not so black and white. Whether or not money gets allocated depends on a multitude of situations and circumstances, which can be affected by a powerful sales professional, as you saw in Thomas's Story.

Be deliberate to connect with everyone. You never know who is and/or who will become a prospect in the future.

Jorge Lopez: Equal Opportunity Attention Giver

Jorge's approach to sales was a masterclass in relationship building. What was his strategy? To become what he called a "professional hall wanderer," a role he embraced with both dedication and finesse.

"If it's Tuesday, it must be Baptist," Jorge would say, referring to his weekly visits to Baptist Hospital. For a full year, Jorge committed to this routine, strategically appearing in hallways and common areas, timing his visits to coincide with breaks and lunch hours.

What set Jorge apart was his commitment to connecting with everyone, not just the decision-makers. "I knew everybody in that place," he'd tell me. "Parking attendants, janitors, everybody." In Jorge's view, every interaction was valuable, potentially planting seeds for future opportunities.

This approach paid dividends in unexpected ways. Years later, during a visit to a hospital a few miles away, the director of Radiology Imaging recognized Jorge. Turns out, this executive had once been an orderly with whom Jorge had taken the time to chat years before. It was a powerful reminder of Jorge's philosophy of treating everyone with respect, granting them his full presence regardless of their role or circumstance.

But perhaps the most impressive result of Jorge's strategy was breaking into his largest account, Baptist Hospital, where his competitor had a longtime stronghold. After a year of consistent presence and relationship building, Jorge's patience paid off. The section chief, now firmly in Jorge's corner, gave him the opening he needed: "Jorge, these guys, your competitors, have pissed me off for the last time. I think your opportunity has come."

It was the culmination of Jorge's long-term strategy. All those casual conversations and "chance" encounters weren't just friendly gestures—they were deliberate moves in a game of authentic connection that spanned years, resulting in a business relationship that would last three decades.

Jorge's approach wasn't just about making a sale. It was about integrating himself into the fabric of these institutions. As he often said, "Luck is nothing more than having preparation and established relationships—everything that comes together when an opportunity is presented to you. Be open and talk to everyone, no matter their job."

In Jorge's world, every interaction held potential, every relationship was an investment. It wasn't just sales; it was a comprehensive strategy of connection and patience that consistently yielded remarkable results. His success was a testament to the power of genuine relationships and the long-term value of treating everyone with equal respect and interest.

Jorge's story illustrates how consistent presence and genuine connection build trust over time. This same patient, strategic approach is crucial when dealing with challenging customers. Let me be crystal clear: I'm not advocating for anyone to accept abuse or tolerate toxic behavior. However, some of your most valuable customer relationships might require extra patience and persistence to develop.

Consider that many difficult executives have earned their positions despite (or sometimes because of) their challenging personalities. They are often brilliant at what they do, and their demanding nature might stem from high standards or past disappointments with vendors. The key is distinguishing between someone who is merely challenging and someone who is truly toxic.

When you encounter a demanding or seemingly unapproachable customer, ask yourself the following questions:

➤ Are they difficult with everyone, or just with vendors?

➤ Do they deliver on their commitments despite their tough exterior?

➤ Can you spot moments of fairness or reasonableness beneath the gruff demeanor?

➤ Are their high standards tied to legitimate business concerns?

If you sense that there is potential for a professional relationship beneath the challenging exterior, persistence might be worth your while. Your next steps are:

➤ Showing up consistently, even when it's uncomfortable.

➤ Delivering on every promise, no matter how small.

➤ Maintaining professionalism even in tense moments.

➤ Standing your ground respectfully when necessary.

➤ Finding appropriate ways to add value between sales cycles.

Building Trust with Difficult Customers: A Story of Persistence

Let me share another story from Thomas (whom you met earlier in the book), that perfectly illustrates the power of building trust with even the most challenging customers. Early in his career at Siemens, Thomas encountered Bill (not his real name), a biomedical director known throughout the industry for his volatile temperament. He had a reputation for screaming at vendors and even at his own staff. The mere mention of his name made seasoned sales professionals wince.

Thomas's first memorable interaction with Bill came during his first September 30th fiscal year close. He needed Bill's signature on a point-of-sale agreement for a dual-source CT scanner. Thomas waited outside Bill's office in the pouring rain, ending up completely drenched in his suit by the time Bill arrived. Something shifted in that moment—perhaps seeing Thomas so committed that he was willing to get soaked by the rain sparked a hint of respect.

But the real breakthrough came during a negotiation involving their Siemens service director, Don. They had made significant price concessions to secure Bill's business, reducing existing prices by ten percent. After Don made the concession, Thomas did something unexpected. He turned to Bill and said, "Now I need to hear from you that when the discussion comes up about whether to buy Siemens, GE, or Phillips, you'll be a proponent for the Siemens offer because of what we're doing."

Bill was visibly uncomfortable. "I don't usually express preferences," he said. "I just say whether something works or not." But Thomas stood firm, insisting that if they were making these concessions, they needed his advocacy in return.

This moment marked a turning point. Bill began seeing them differently, recognizing that they weren't just another vendor making empty promises—they were partners invested in providing superior service and technology to his health system.

The true test came a year later when Thomas discovered they were about to lose a deal for CT scanners at the largest hospital in the health system. He went directly to Bill, explaining that they were about to make a purchase of a CT scanner without upgrade capability, but that Siemens could provide a better, upgradeable CT scanner for a slightly larger investment. Bill, in his characteristic style, began talking to himself about the shortsightedness of buying cheap equipment only to have to replace it later. He marched into a meeting with the COO and shut down the competitor's purchase. Siemens won the deal.

Yes, Bill still yelled at Thomas sometimes—once for twenty straight minutes while a hospital director watched in horror. But at the end of his tirade, Thomas simply said, "We'll make this right, like we always do." Because by then, they had built a foundation of trust. Bill knew they would deliver.

The lesson from Thomas's story is powerful: In sales, you'll encounter people who seem impenetrable, who test your resolve and resilience. They are often difficult with everyone, not just you. But if you can be one of the rare professionals who can transform that relationship and build genuine trust, you create an ally for life. It requires patience, persistence, and the courage to stand your ground while remaining respectful.

Remember, building trust isn't about being subservient or always saying yes. It's about showing up consistently, delivering on your promises, and having the confidence to engage in honest, direct dialogue. When you can master this delicate dance, you separate yourself from the pack and create relationships that transcend typical vendor-client dynamics.

However, if you encounter behavior that crosses the line into abuse, discrimination, or harassment, that's different. It is crucial to understand that no sale is worth your dignity or well-being. There's a clear distinction between a demanding customer who needs to be won over and someone who's truly toxic.

The key is to be strategic about where you invest your persistence. When you identify a challenging but potentially valuable relationship, create a long-term plan for building trust. Accept that it might take longer than usual, but the payoff—a strong relationship with a formerly "impossible" customer—can be worth the extra effort.

Whether you're building relationships throughout an organization like Jorge or working to transform a challenging relationship into a powerful partnership like Thomas, the fundamental principle remains the same: Success in sales often comes down to genuine relationship building, strategic persistence, and the wisdom to know where to invest your time and energy. Some of your most loyal advocates might start as your toughest customers, and some of your biggest opportunities might come from unexpected places. The key is maintaining your professionalism, authenticity, and commitment to building genuine connections, no matter who you're dealing with.

Identifying Roles of People in the Process of Prospecting

In order to be prepared for conversations, it is important to identify the roles to prospect. You need to know if the person you are talking to is a gatekeeper, an advisor or coach, an influencer, or a decision-maker.

Gatekeepers: These are the people responsible for controlling access to a decision-maker or a department. Gatekeepers play a crucial role in managing the flow of information, requests, and communication within an organization.

Examples of gatekeepers in business include receptionists or administrative/executive assistants who screen calls, emails, and visitors, who at times also manage the schedules and priorities of top-level executives, determining who gets access to them and when.

In some cases, gatekeepers may also be seen as barriers to communication or progress, particularly when they are overly restrictive in granting access or when they lack the knowledge to accurately assess the importance of a request.

Be open, kind, and connect with gatekeepers; they can be a blockade or a resourceful ally in your journey.

Advisors/Coaches: In the context of the sales process, an advisor or coach within the customer's organization plays a crucial role in guiding the decision-making process and influencing the outcome of a sale. These are key people with whom a strong sales professional works to co-create the sale completion.

These individuals may not have the final say in purchasing decisions, but their opinions and recommendations carry significant weight with the decision-makers. These are the people from within the account who can help guide you, orient you, and navigate the dominant strategy with the customer to get to the close.

Advisors or coaches within the customer's organization can take on various roles, such as:

➤ Technical Advisors: These individuals have in-depth knowledge of the company's technical requirements, systems, and processes. They can provide valuable insights into how a product or service will fit into the organization's existing infrastructure and workflows. They provide valuable feedback on user requirements, preferences, and potential adoption challenges.

➤ Financial Advisors: These individuals are responsible for assessing the financial impact of a purchase, including budgeting, ROI analysis, and cost-benefit evaluations. They may work closely with the purchasing department to ensure that any acquisition aligns with the company's financial goals and constraints.

➤ Administrative or Strategic Advisors: These individuals review contracts and agreements, and make sure that terms and conditions of a sale comply with the organization's requirements. They are often senior managers or executives who evaluate how a purchase aligns with the company's overall strategic objectives. They consider factors such as competitive advantage, long-term growth, and market positioning when making recommendations.

To effectively navigate the sales process, it is essential for salespeople to identify and engage with the advisors and coaches within the customer's organization. Building strong relationships with these individuals can provide valuable insights into the customer's needs, priorities, and decision-making processes. By addressing their concerns and leveraging their influence, salespeople can increase the likelihood of a successful sale and build long-term partnerships with the customer.

Influencers: In the sales process, an influencer is an individual who has the power to sway or impact the purchasing decision, even though they may not be the final decision-maker. Influencers can come from various departments or levels within the customer's organization and can significantly impact the success or failure of a sale. They shape perceptions within the customer organization and can champion a solution if they strongly believe in a product or service.

If your influencer is also a coach, then you are in great shape.

That combination will not only guide you and inform you, but they can also be a champion for your solution inside the customer's organization.

Decision-Makers: In the sales process, decision-makers are the individuals within the customer's organization who have the ultimate authority to approve or reject a purchase. They are responsible for making the final decision on whether to buy a product or service, and their choices are typically based on a combination of factors, including the company's needs, budget, and strategic goals.

> **A brief note/disclaimer:** Gatekeepers, coaches, influencers, and decision-makers can come from the administrative, technical, or financial domain of a business. That said, I have never encountered a situation where the financial decision didn't take priority. If the money isn't available, the deal doesn't work. It's that simple. However, sometimes the funds can be found even if there wasn't a budget allocation, and most of the time, it's a powerful relationship with the "right" prospect that makes for such unusual circumstances.

I urge you to do the research on every account to get an understanding of the players involved, their level of influence, and ultimately how the purchase process is completed. It seems straightforward and obvious, but this is a major blind spot for many sales professionals. I am amazed how many experienced salespeople don't know the details when it comes to the process at their accounts. Once you are clear on the process to completion, you can reverse engineer which prospects need your attention and which human beings in the organization are required to buy in to your product or service in order for the deal to happen. This will define who you need to call on, connect with, and progress in the sales process to bring it to completion.

Prospecting Is Assessing Viability and the Art of Seduction

Does the person(s) with whom you are engaging qualify as a viable prospect?

Do they have authority, a need, a willingness to listen, and the funds to move forward?

If yes, then your job is to create their curiosity. A hint of tension is good here. It is wonderful to leave the customer feeling interested and curious. Creating this tension (or seduction) is an art. Be mindful of the pitfall of answering too many questions. We are conditioned to answer questions, especially when we are trying to gain favor with a prospect. Be careful here. Don't do it. You don't know enough yet. You get to prepare for the qualifying meeting once you have completed the prospecting conversation. And best of all, you get to create a hint of curiosity for your customer which leaves them longing for more. This is the magic that will powerfully set you up for the qualifying meeting.

Just like a good movie that has a sequel, you leave the theater satisfied and excited with anticipation of the upcoming film. Leaving your customer curious works wonders for creating their context for you—how they approach the upcoming meeting, their mood, their willingness to engage and listen.

A Tactical Superpower

There is a wonderful tactic that I highly recommend for salespeople who are interested in setting themselves up for the most effective qualifying meeting possible.

Here it is: Give your customer homework!

This tactic does two things. If you do it well, you will set up the customer to know what they need to know to be engaged in conversation with you; they will be curious and fully present during the meeting. Second, you can identify the efficacy of your sales process thus far by whether you have established enough relevance with the customer that they will want to take some form of action on their own.

If your customer completes the homework, you know they are invested. This puts you in good shape for the next part of the sales process.

What kind of homework do you give to customers? Ask them to do something for the upcoming meeting. Make sure it is relevant and pragmatic for them and for you. Just like when you are interested in something and you are willing to do a little bit of digging for information, the same goes for most people. Think of the last time you were willing to do some research before making a big decision or purchase.

One example of this is that you ask them to gather data that could be relevant to a problem you can help them solve. A specific situation from my experience was to ask the Director of Radiology how much backlog of patients they had experienced in the last six months for their MRI scanner and how much they budgeted for billing per scan. This is a great example of a way to gather information that you can use to set up the presentation of your offer.

If a customer doesn't complete the homework, it's a sign that you haven't sufficiently connected with them. Every breakdown in the sales process can usually be traced back to a misstep in an earlier stage.

Quick reminder. Don't sell yet. It's like throwing a can of paint on the wall and assuming you will make beautiful art. While it may happen for a select few, the likelihood is small, so be patient and get ready.

If you have gotten this far, well done! Next is the qualifying part of the sales process and when things tend to get much more interesting.

KEY TAKEAWAYS

1. Be prepared for the conversation
   - ➤ Explore your prospect online through web searches and social media.
   - ➤ Understand the person's history as much as you can, as well as the company history, mission, and values.
   - ➤ Know some fundamentals about the industry and current events/trends.
   - ➤ Identify the customer role/influence in the organization when you are prospecting.

2. Be intentional and authentic in creating connection and establishing credibility
   - ➤ Check in on your mood. Be intentional with it.
   - ➤ Establish credibility.

3. Assess viability of prospect
   - ➤ Look for authority, need, urgency, funds, and willingness to listen.
   - ➤ Don't sell prematurely—focus on curiosity and rapport.
   - ➤ Use small "homework" requests to gauge and produce engagement.
   - ➤ The outcome of prospecting is simple: set up a qualifying meeting.

CHAPTER 11

Qualifying

Qualifying is a crucial step in the sales process that follows prospecting. At this stage, you've already identified a viable prospect. The goal of qualifying is to dig deeper, gather more specific information, and determine if there's a good fit between your offering and the prospect's needs. This chapter will guide you through the qualifying process, helping you to effectively assess opportunities and set the stage for a successful sale.

The Map: A Structure for Effective Qualifying

The Map is a powerful framework for qualifying prospects. It's important to understand that The Map isn't just a set of questions to ask; it's a structure that guides you toward your ultimate destination in the sales process. That destination is gathering enough information to create a workable presentation or demonstration, which in turn allows you to move toward closing the sale.

By using The Map, you're not just collecting data—you're strategically assembling the building blocks for your next steps in the sales process. Each element of The Map (which probes the Who, What,

When, Where, Why) contributes vital information that will shape your presentation, help you address the prospect's specific needs, and ultimately, position you to close the deal.

The Map: Who, What, When, Where, Why

To effectively qualify a prospect, thoroughly explore each aspect of The Map. Using the five elements, you'll gather the insights needed to create a presentation that resonates deeply with your prospect. This tailored approach significantly increases your chances of moving smoothly from presentation to closing the deal.

The exercise of going through each of these aspects will help you gather comprehensive information about your prospect, their needs, the relevant content and context of the customer, their situation, and how your product and/or service fits. Let's break it down:

Who: This is where we start. We start with the "Who" because you are framing the rest of The Map to this person(s) in order to get buy-in or alignment, which is fundamental to a transaction or closing a deal. Orienting to your customer so that you gain an audience with the key stakeholders is necessary. Discovering Who that is, is Step 1 of The Map.

Define and choose the key stakeholders in your audience. Focus on the key decision-maker(s) as you contemplate the following:

➤ Who is impacted by the situation within the customer organization?

➤ Who are the key players in the decision-making process? Note: Finding a financial decision-maker is ideal. A financial influencer is second best.

Sometimes, your prospect isn't the financial decision-maker or a key financial influencer. In these cases, you need to navigate the qualifying phase to reach stakeholders who have real decision-making power or influence.

Your goal? Ask questions, share stories, and make requests that prompt your prospect to engage with these key players. By doing this, you'll co-create narratives that spark interest and demonstrate value to the decision makers.

The endgame is twofold: First, capture their interest, then gain direct access to these financial decision-makers or influencers. This allows you to qualify and present your product or service, aiming for their approval. Keep in mind, direct access is always best.

Remember, decisions are always personal. Consider the following factors:

> Identity—how does the customer see themselves in their role? What could make them look good to their peers and leaders? What could you do that prevents them from looking bad? Everyone, at one point or another, more often than not, is looking to improve their identity so that they can continue to grow, evolve, get promoted, etc.

> Their boss's approval

> Family considerations

> Desire for autonomy

> Legacy concerns

> Power dynamics

> Political considerations within the organization

What: Explore "What" matters most to your prospects:

> What do they care about? Make it as personal and specific as you can.

➤ What would make them look good or help them avoid looking bad?

➤ What keeps them up at night? What isn't working in their business?

➤ In what ways are they losing money, revenue, resources, market share, etc.?

➤ If the customer has transacted within your market segment in the past, with what competitor did they work? What commitments do they currently have within your segment (previous equipment or services already in place) that work (or are in conflict) with what you are proposing?

➤ What are their current behavior, process, or transaction patterns in the marketplace relative to your product or service (e.g., their purchasing process, the kinds of vendors they work with)?

➤ Learn their purchasing process! This is essential for salespeople and for any well-run revenue-generating team for the sake of forecasting clarity. Find out what thresholds and approvals are needed to bring the sales process to a close as you qualify. In my experience, many salespeople are somewhat apprehensive about exploring this. My recommendation (from experience) is that you ask your customer coach/advisor, when you have established enough rapport that you feel connected to them, and they will tell you the truth. If your customer knows you well enough, they will share this with you without trepidation.

When: Timing can be crucial in qualifying a prospect. You need to dig into the following:

➤ Is there a specific horizon of time that matters to the customer and if so, why is it important?

➤ Is there a sense of urgency for them to move forward now, as opposed to later?

➤ Is there a narrative around the timing that makes the transaction mutually beneficial?

➤ Once again, it's crucial to understand the customer's purchasing process, including (when applicable) budgeting, approval process, pricing thresholds, board meeting dates, who must sign off on project, computer application for sign-offs, etc. Again, I recommend you discover this with an advisor/coach customer.

Understanding the "When" helps you align your sales process with the prospect's timeline, create a sense of urgency in your presentation, and plan your closing strategy.

Let me share a personal example that really drives home how timing can make or break a deal. I had a customer who was itching to open his next imaging center. Sounds great, right? But here's the catch—he was gun-shy because his previous center had hit a wall with construction issues and therefore, delayed opening. This was costly and painful. This guy was worried sick about putting the same kind of budget strain on his organization again. They lost out on several months of forecasted revenue in the last project, which placed a tremendous burden on their executive team with the board.

We brought in our project management team, who then pulled in local contractors and even got city approvals to smooth the path. We were basically paving the way for this customer to feel comfortable moving forward.

The timing implications from his previous experience had created some serious resistance. But by addressing those concerns head-on and showing we could manage the timeline effectively, my organization was able to overcome that resistance. We turned a potential "not now" into a "let's do this."

This just goes to show: Timing isn't just about when they want to buy. It's about understanding their past experiences, current hesitations, and future concerns. When you see the full picture, you can tailor your approach to overcome timing-related objections and keep the deal moving forward.

Last, but certainly not least, there are your own and your company's considerations as it relates to time.

➤ How does the timing of the deal matter to you?

➤ By when do you want or need the deal to close?

➤ Can you relate that to the customer's needs in some way?

This is where salespeople can go off the deep end, so I highly recommend being true to yourself. You need to take a hard look at your motivations. Is this something you need to fulfill your forecast? Are you feeling the heat to hit your numbers?

Here's the thing: Desperation has a funny way of seeping into your interactions, and believe me, customers can smell it a mile away. It's like trying to hide a skunk in your briefcase—it just doesn't work. So, I want you to do something that might feel a bit uncomfortable. Take a step back and notice how you're feeling. Are you clutching onto this opportunity like it's a life raft in choppy waters? Or can you hold it lightly, like a butterfly that might flit away at any moment?

If you're feeling that desperation creeping in, take a deep breath. Remember, your worth isn't tied to this one deal. Your value as a salesperson—and as a human being—doesn't hinge on whether this particular prospect signs on the dotted line.

Try to approach each interaction with a sense of curiosity and openness. You're not there to push a product; you're there to explore a potential fit.

I always remind my team that being in a state of despair isn't pretty and it won't help you. When you're not desperate, you can be present, and you make better decisions. You ask better questions. You listen more carefully. And ironically, this relaxed, authentic approach often leads to better outcomes.

So, as you're working through The Map and qualifying your prospects, keep checking in with yourself. Stay true to who you are.

Friendly Reminder (from Part 1 of this book): While closing deals undoubtedly impacts your sales results, being fully present and curious throughout this process is crucial. Approach this phase with intention and mindfulness. I often advise holding the outcome lightly. The path to achieving your desired results lies in embodying an energized, authentic state—free from the grip of fear about the unknown or potential loss. Your demeanor is paramount to your success, and that's entirely within your control. Protect it fiercely.

Where: Consider the physical space and organizational context when filling out the "Where" aspect of The Map.

> ➤ Does geographic location matter to the prospect or the solution? (For example, room size and proximity to power for equipment sales.)

> ➤ Does the amount of space matter to the customer?

> ➤ Is your qualification process happening in a space that is conducive to successful communication? (For example, does the office, boardroom, or meeting room have sufficient space for everyone and a comfortable place to sit?)

Be mindful to create an environment where your communication can be heard and where your audience will be optimized for paying attention to you.

Why: The final section of The Map is to understand the deeper motivations and consequences, the "Why."

➤ Why does this need matter to them?

➤ Why are these problems creating concern, friction, or fear right now?

➤ Why is solving this problem critical to achieving their business goals?

➤ Why would failing to act—or staying in the status quo—be quote unacceptable or costly for them?

➤ Is there a way to help the customers achieve their goal across multiple departments or problems, such that one or two actions (as part of working with you) cascades into several improvements organizationally, operationally, and/or financially?

This next example shows the power and impact that a relationship with an influencer/coach can have on your career (and life) as you qualify. This is a story of how listening to your truth, being authentic, cultivating rapport, and taking rigorous action with courage can transform the impossible into reality.

A Tipping Point in My Career

When I first learned that Siemens had been locked out of a major regional health system's molecular imaging contract for five long years, I felt the ground give way beneath me. As a salesperson based in Orlando, this news was more than just a setback—it was a potential career-ender. With only one other major hospital system in the area, which I had already fully penetrated, my options for hitting my numbers had just drastically narrowed. I had spent the previous two years investing in relationship building with physicians, technologists, and administrators throughout that health system. The flagship hospital is one mile away from my house. These people became a part of my community. I opened doors for several of my colleagues to foster relationships in their modality over these years. Those other modalities were all chosen to be on contract but for my modality, Siemens was excluded. I was dumbfounded, outraged, and sad. I felt betrayed and heartbroken.

The contracting process occured only once every five years. Siemens had rarely been selected for any modality. The process was rigorous and extensive, with a large committee of clinical, techincal, and administrative members evaluating vendors through a formal Request for Proposal. Each modality had its own group of experts who ultimately voted to determine which vendors would be included. That vote was scheduled for the evening of June 6, 2013, after months of deliberation. Once finalized, the supply chain team would move forward to solidify the terms and sign off on the vendors—those who would have a "license to hunt" for the next five years.

I will never forget it; it was the morning of June 7, 2013. I was in Vancouver at the annual trade show for Molecular Imaging. It was a gorgeous day. I got the call and my heart sank into my chest. The stakeholders with whom I had built rapport and who were a part of the Molecular Imaging committee were absent from the voting. How did this happen? Maybe one was sick or maybe they were dealing with a department emergency. What were the chances?

As I sat with the weight of this reality, I cried. I confided in my boss and heard the words I needed to hear. "If anyone can do this, it's you. Go make them change the vote." Easy for him to say! I knew that this vendor selection process had been in place for decades and that the decision had never before been overturned after the vote.

This organization was famous for their rigor and process. My boss's boss suggested that I stand down, "to not cry over spilled milk," as he was overjoyed at the thought of the modalities that had made it on to the agreement. It felt impossible and yet, a flicker of determination ignited within me.

So I got to work. I chose to go for it and to take my boss's suggestion, while ignoring the big boss's fear that I would create disruption. I tapped into the relationships within the company who supported me, including my local team, and strategically moved forward with the objective to change the contract. I started by identifying and connecting with every possible stakeholder who might have an influence on the contract. I met with doctors, imaging technologists, administrators—anyone who would give me the time of day. I had solid relationships and all of them were willing to go to bat to include Siemens for Molecular Imaging.

What I discovered was that while the supply chain team was fixated on having two vendor options for each modality, they were missing a crucial piece of information for Molecular Imaging. For one equipment category (a hybrid nuclear medicine and CT scanner, SPECT CT) that made up the bulk of the contract's value, they actually had no viable second option. By insisting on a dual-source approach across the board, one of the two vendors they chose didn't have the type of technology they were looking for. They were unwittingly backing themselves into a sole-source situation for their most important Molecular Imaging purchase.

Armed with this insight, I knew I had an opportunity. But I also knew that approaching the supply chain team directly was unlikely to yield results. They had no existing relationship with me, no technical knowledge, and in the midst of an active RFP process, they were wary of any perceived vendor influence.

So instead, I leveraged the relationships I had spent years

cultivating. I worked with the lead physician, a longtime advocate, to help craft the message. I coordinated with leaders and administration, who had the ear of the supply chain team, to deliver the insight at just the right moment.

And slowly but surely, the tide began to turn. The supply chain executive, confronted with the reality of his SPECT CT situation, realized that including Siemens as a third option was not only acceptable, it was necessary to meet the contract's two-vendor requirement.

Toward the end of August, when the final five-year contract was published, with Siemens officially invited to bid on Molecular Imaging, I could hardly believe it. It was a first. I was elated. This felt like a testament to the power of self-trust, persistence, strategic thinking, and above all, the deep qualitative listening I had done for the years of rapport building.

In the years that followed, that single contract win transformed my career. I went from scrambling for every small opportunity to being the top salesperson in the US, with a reliable pipeline of business from a marquee account.

But more than that, it taught me an invaluable lesson about the true meaning of qualifying. It's not just about checking boxes or gathering surface-level information. It's about digging deeper, understanding the human dynamics and motivations at play, and finding ways to align your solution with the customer's true needs— even when they themselves might not yet fully grasp them.

Of course, none of this would have been possible without the years of groundwork I had laid beforehand. The trusted relationships with physicians and technologists, the intimate knowledge of the account's history and priorities—these were the foundations upon which my qualifying efforts could bear fruit.

And that, perhaps, is the most important takeaway of all: Effective qualifying doesn't start when an RFP is released or a contract comes up for renewal. It starts with the very first handshake, the very first conversation. It starts with a commitment to showing up, again and again, to learn and understand and add value, long before you ever make an ask. Dig your well before you need to drink from it.

Because in the end, that's what sets the great salespeople apart. It's not just their tactical skills or their product knowledge, but their willingness to invest in relationships, to listen with empathy and curiosity, and to always, always keep showing up. Even in the face of seemingly impossible odds.

Be intentional and authentic as you engage in the prospecting part of the sales process whether you are live or virtual. Most of us are scared of meeting new people, even if it's just a flash of fear that subsides quickly. That's okay. How you enter a conversation matters. Your mood will be the first thing people notice after they see you.

Using The Map in Qualification

As you work through The Map during your qualification process:

1. Take detailed notes on each aspect (Who, What, When, Where, Why).
2. Look for connections between different areas. For example, does the "Who" influence the "Why"?
3. Pay attention to both explicit statements and implicit cues from your prospect.
4. Use this information to assess whether your solution is truly a good fit for the prospect's needs and context.
5. Identify any gaps in your understanding that need to be filled before moving forward.

Post-Qualification Analysis

After you gather information using The Map:

1. Review your notes and identify the key points in each category.
2. Assess the viability of the prospect based on this comprehensive view.
3. Determine if you need any additional information before moving to the next stage.
4. Begin to formulate ideas on how your solution can best address the prospect's specific situation. Answer the following question: Why will the customer choose your solution? And, why now?
5. Consider how you'll present your solution in light of the information you've gathered.

Remember, effective qualification sets the stage for a powerful presentation on your product or service. By thoroughly understanding your prospect through The Map, you'll be well-equipped to tailor your approach and offer a solution that truly resonates with their needs and context.

Qualifying using The Map approach allows you to gain a deep, multifaceted understanding of your prospect. This comprehensive view enables you to assess whether there's a genuine fit between your offering and the prospect's needs, setting the foundation for a successful sale. By diligently working through the Who, What, When, Where, and Why, you'll be well-prepared to move forward in the sales process with confidence and clarity.

KEY TAKEAWAYS

1. Use The Map
   - ➤ Qualifying means digging deeper with *Who, What, When, Where, Why.*
   - ➤ Focus on key decision-makers and what really matters to them.

2. Stay Curious and Present
   - ➤ Ask open-ended questions to uncover real needs and motivations.
   - ➤ Hold the outcome lightly—curiosity builds trust, desperation erodes it.

3. Post-Qualification Analysis
   - ➤ Review your notes and highlight the most important insights.
   - ➤ Look for gaps you still need to fill before moving forward.
   - ➤ Use what you've learned to shape a tailored presentation that resonates.

CHAPTER 12

Presenting

Once you gather the relevant information during the qualifying phase of the sales process, you are ready to design and craft the narratives of your product and/or service for the customer into a cohesive order for the presentation.

The purpose of this phase of the sales process is to communicate your offer and how it fits the customer's needs. The intention is to gain acceptance from the customer so that they are ready to move forward with a decision to buy.

Before you get started, do the following exercise to get ready.

EXERCISE

Focus Your Presentation

In order to focus your presentation, pause now and take the time to answer the following questions.

1. What mood do you want to create during the presentation?

2. How do you want the audience to feel?
3. What do you want them to remember and know about you and the product/service that you are presenting?
4. Who do you need to be to create the above?
5. What do you need to do to create the above?

Giving yourself the space to focus your way of BEing for when you present will help guide your intuition as you craft and make your presentation.

Designing Your Presentation

As I qualify and gather the intelligence I need to create a presentation that resonates, I always start with the audience.

Step 1: Identify who the key person(s) is—list the stakeholders and choose the key decision-maker and/or influencer(s). Ideally, I like to have specific knowledge of the persons I will be presenting to and I pick one or two people at whom I focus the presentation.

Note that the financial stakeholder almost always must be accounted for in your thinking. If you don't have a sound financial case in your presentation, the likelihood of closing a transaction is much lower.

Step 2: Draw a plot line.

The plot line is a way to look at the basic structure you want to create within a presentation.

The exposition is the introduction where you distinguish the set, setting, actors/stakeholders, etc. This is where you set the mood and the tone of the upcoming space and time. Be deliberate in constituting what you want to create in the experience.

BASIC PLOT DIAGRAM

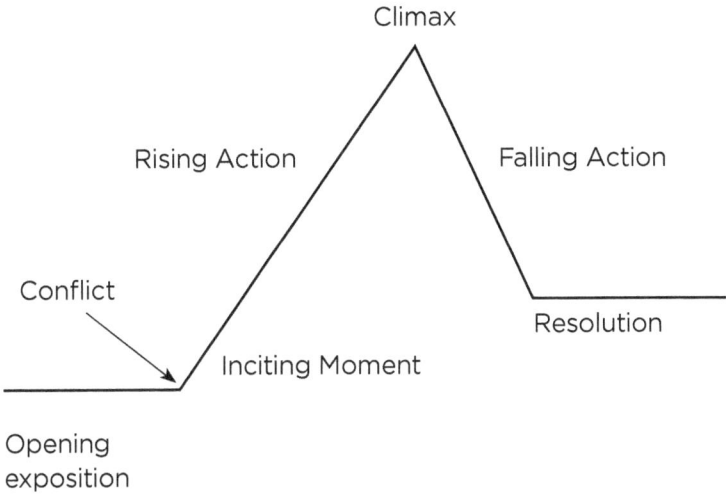

The conflict or the inciting moment is where you capture the audience. Like in any movie, the way the audience is hooked into the story and why they pay attention moving forward depends on how well you have captured the conflict for them. It is something they feel in their body resulting from a thought. Usually, there is tension and just like you, they want to see how the story unfolds because it matters to them personally. As you tell the story, you bring clarity and color in the rising action and then you declare the climax, which if done well, creates a surge of energy because your solution addresses or even solves the customers' conflict. Finally, the resolution (or happy ending) that becomes available from transacting with you will emerge and a new realm of possibilities that addresses their desires is born.

Defining the conflict is one of the most important parts of your presentation. If you do this well, you will have the audience's attention.

In order to best define the conflict and how I can create a resolution with my product or service, I follow the simple framework of The Map from the previous chapter on qualifying. You want to know the Who, What, When, Where, and Why of their situation as part of the Rising Action.

The rising action is a crucial part of a story's plot structure. It is the series of events that build tension, introduce conflicts, and develop characters after the initial exposition.

Typically, the rising action:

➤ Follows the inciting incident

➤ Presents obstacles and challenges for the protagonist (your key stakeholder(s))

➤ Increases the stakes and complexity of the story

➤ Develops relationships between characters

➤ Builds suspense and engagement

➤ Leads up to the climax of the story

Use The Map for Presenting

Who: Define and choose the Who's Who in the audience. Focus on the key stakeholder(s) as you contemplate the following inquiries. Who is impacted by the situation within the customer organization?

What: What do they care about? Make it as personal and specific as you can.

Note: Decisions are always personal. What are the motivations: money, budgets, identity, their boss's approval, family, autonomy, legacy, power, politics?

What would make them look good or avoid looking bad?

What keeps them up at night? What isn't working in their business? Where are they losing money, revenue, resources, market share, etc.?

What are they already committed to that works or doesn't work with what you are proposing?

What are their current behavior, process, or transaction patterns in the marketplace relative to your product of service; i.e., their purchasing process, the kinds of vendors with which they work, etc.?

When: Is there a specific time that matters to the customer, and if so, why is it important?

Is there a sense of urgency for them to move forward now, as opposed to later?

By when do you need the deal to close? And can you relate that to the customer's needs in some way?

Where: Does geographic location matter?

Does the amount of space matter to the customer?

Is your presentation in a space that is conducive to a successful communication?

Why: Why does this matter to them at a human and busines business level? Why are these issues creating tension, concern, or urgency right now? Why is solving this problem essential to meeting their goals? What is the customer's story about their need? What are their conditions of satisfaction to solve their problem(s) or fear(s)?

What is the customer's story of the consequences of not addressing their problem(s)?

Is there a way to help the customers achieve their goal across multiple departments, problems such that one or two actions (as part of working with you) cascades into several improvements organizationally, operationally, and/or financially?

Crafting Your Presentation

Once you have completed the inquiries in The Map, take a few deep breaths.

1. Write a phrase or several phrases that define the conflict.
2. Select a few key pieces from The Map that could be helpful in defining "why you" and "why now" (from the customer's point of view).

    The "why you" and "why now" helps you define the climax and creates the resolution of your presentation; after all, a presentation is a story told in front of an audience—how you and/ or your solution helps the customer resolve their need.

    This is how you declare what makes you marginally better than everyone else—it is the magic (and relief) you bring to them, being the climax in the story or plotline and co-creating a world where your product/service is the resolution to the customer's conflict or problem(s). Note, your product or service doesn't need to be substantially better than the competition's, just better enough that you, your product, or service are assessed to be a better alternative than any other or to doing nothing at all.

3. Confirm the products/services in your portfolio that address the customer conflict as this will be the solution (product/ service) that you will propose in the climax that feeds the resolution.
4. Describe their situation and the consequences—the rising action—such that the customer sees that you have a deep understanding of their operation and needs. This is your chance to create and relieve tension through your storytelling. If you qualified well and have an energetic communication style, your customer will be paying attention and learning during your presentation. People love a good story. If it's

relevant to them, if it helps them address conflict or concerns (remember, this has to be personal and meaningful to them), they will listen.

Note: It has to be personal; otherwise, the likelihood is low that they will care enough about what you are presenting, and they will likely be listening to the chatter in their minds instead of you. How many times have you been in a presentation where you were bored senseless and scrolling through social media from the side of your eye to get through the hour?

    a. I suggest clearly defining the 2 or 3 key messages you want your customer to remember. The likelihood is that they will remember ten percent of what you say, at best. So, be intentional and repeat these key messages two or three times for them. Repetition works.

    b. When a story hits home, it makes people feel feelings. Craft your story to produce feelings. It works. If you see people's cheeks blushing or eyes peering at you, you nailed it.

5. Define the possibilities that will exist for the customer once they transact with you. That is the "happily ever after" moment in the movie or the book. This is a vision that you can co-create with them. Ideally, if you do this well, you cast a vision for possibilities for their organization that cannot exist without your product or service.

6. Write your introduction.

⚠ MINDFULNESS ALERT ⚠

Be intentional about your mood, who you want to BE that day and what you want the audience to know about you. This is a superpower of effective sales professionals.

7. Practice, practice, practice. Make it yours. Make it seamless. I strongly prefer presenting without memorizing or reading every word. When I hear memorized or read presentations, I feel like I am listening to a robotic automaton and most often, I tune out. I like to speak with and be with the audience throughout my presentation. In my experience, this method has a much higher likelihood of resonating with the audience and progressing your sales process.

When it comes to creating and designing a slide deck for a presentation, I subscribe to the MVP (minimum viable product) philosophy. Keep the volume of slides and the words on the slides themselves to a minimum. I imagine that you have experienced death by PowerPoint yourself. I know that I have and don't recommend it to anyone, especially if you want the audience to walk away remembering much of what you shared.

Use a slide to show something (e.g., a diagram to show trends or metrics, a photo, etc.) that you can't describe as well in speaking. A picture is worth a thousand words, after all. Use minimal language on a slide. Only include what is useful to you as the presenter, so you do not take the audience's attention away from you. If the audience sees words on a slide, their attention will likely be averted away from you to read the words. If you are speaking while they are reading your slide, they are not likely to be listening to you. I prefer to be the center of attention (no surprises there), connecting with my audience, so I have a minor disdain for unnecessary words and slides in presenting.

During the Presentation

Set yourself up for success ahead of your presentation with the following steps:

1. Confirm that you and your space have the set and setting you need for a viable presentation to the audience. Take care of your body; get good rest and proper nutrition the day before and day of the presentation. Confirm the workability of audio, video, and seating for all attendees.

2. Be intentional, constitute who you want to be in the room that day, get present to that way of being, be clear about what you want to create with the audience, and *go get 'em.*

3. Gain feedback and intelligence from the presentation. While presenting, be open and available to learn whatever you can from your customer. Create an opportunity for them to give you feedback if that is possible. My personal preference is to have a few moments in the presentation where I ask the audience for their impressions. This is an opportunity to learn about your customer from what they say and how they act.

4. Notice and reflect on how your narrative is landing for the customer.

   a. I highly recommend having other members of your team there to be the eyes and ears, to observe the body language of the audience and notice when their energy goes up and down. Having someone who practices with you and supports you during presentations can be profoundly useful in the moment; for instance, they can give you a gesture to speak up, speed up, or slow down, and be there for the post-presentation debrief. In case you miss something in your presentation, your peers can support you and add that information or remind you to add it in the moment.

   b. Do a post-presentation debrief as soon as possible once you complete the presentation.

After presenting, you might find yourself needing to requalify or fine-tune how you position your product or service for your customer. The feedback you get during the presentation is incredibly valuable, so don't overlook it. You might need to loop back to the qualifying phase, ask more questions, and give additional presentations. This is pretty standard in sales, especially when you're dealing with complex accounts or big-ticket, high-scope deals. Keep revisiting The Map and treat it as a living document. As you learn more about your customer, use that intel to sharpen your offer, refine your pitch, and tailor your presentation. This ongoing process helps you navigate toward closing the deal more effectively.

Objection Handling and Conscious Listening

When customers raise objections—a normal and frequent occurrence in sales—they're providing valuable guidance on what still needs to be qualified or clarified. Objections aren't negative—quite the opposite. They often reveal additional insights into the customer's perspective and concerns. When facing objections, think back to the connecting and qualifying chapters. The key is to maintain an open, rapport-building approach and really listen to their stories. This equips you with the tools to move forward and close.

When a customer has a question or voices an objection, reflect on your commitment to your way of BEing to produce the outcomes you want. Check in with yourself. Are you feeling pressured? Triggered? Are you defensive? Are you making the customer wrong? All of these reactions are normal and while they are valid, they don't create a space of mutual possibility.

When customers raise objections, I highly recommend using the tactics of Conscious Listening.

Conscious Listening is an active and mindful approach to hearing and understanding others. It is a process of listening openly from the mind, heart, and body.

Conscious Listening involves the following:

➤ **Full attention:** Being present and focused on the speaker

➤ **Non-judgment:** Suspending personal biases and preconceptions

➤ **Empathy:** Trying to understand the speaker's perspective and emotions

➤ **Patience:** Allowing the speaker to express themselves fully without interruption

➤ **Awareness:** Noticing both verbal and non-verbal cues

➤ **Reflection:** Considering the meaning behind the words

➤ **Clarification:** Asking thoughtful questions to ensure understanding

➤ **Feedback:** Providing appropriate responses to show engagement

This practice goes beyond simply hearing words. It's about deeply connecting with the speaker and truly comprehending their message.

When the customer tells you something, reconstitute (repeat) what the customer said, such that they hear their message from you. The objective of this is that they feel accepted and gotten.

For example, if the customer says, "I don't like the way the project was designed. It's not optimized for workflow," your response would be as follows: "What I heard you say is that you don't like the way the project was designed and that it isn't optimized for workflow. Did I get that right?"

The customer may come back with more elaboration. Or, they

might say, "Yes, that's right." Either way, your role in the conversation is to listen, accept their feedback, and make sure that the customer feels like you got what they said.

From there, you have a choice in how to move forward. The coherence of your mind, heart, and body is of the essence. Notice your state, your reactivity. If you are open, you will feel a flow to the conversation, not a contraction. You will know what to say because you are available to meet the customer where they are, not make them wrong, and create a way forward together. If you are feeling closed and likely (somewhat) hijacked, it's okay. Remember that you have the tools to shift. Breathe deeply, tap your foot, do whatever works for you to get centered so that you can be present and available for the conversation with the customer as opposed to the amplified dialogue happening in your mind.

From there you might come back with a response such as:

"Thank you for sharing that with me. I understand that the workflow matters to you, and I will have our planners edit the design to address your concerns. That makes a lot of sense. I want you and your workflow to experience a high level of satisfaction. We will get back to you within three business days with a new plan."

Handling objections is an ongoing part of the sales process. Remember, the solutions to any challenge become much more accessible when you're intentional about your way of BEing. By staying present, open, and genuinely attentive to your customer's needs, you are NOT making them wrong; instead, you create an environment where both parties can work together toward a mutually beneficial outcome. This approach not only helps in resolving immediate concerns but also builds trust and strengthens your relationship with the customer, paving the way for long-term success in your sales endeavors.

KEY TAKEAWAYS

1. Focus your presentation before you build it
   - ➤ Define the mood you want to create and how you want the audience to feel.
   - ➤ Decide what you want them to remember about you and your offer.
   - ➤ Ask: Who do I need to BE and what will I DO to create that outcome?

2. Design with the audience and a story arc
   - ➤ Start with the Who—identify key decision-makers/ influencers (especially financial).
   - ➤ Use a simple plot line: exposition → conflict → rising action → climax (your solution) → resolution.
   - ➤ Make the conflict personal and meaningful to them.

3. Use The Map to tailor the message
   - ➤ Build your narrative from Who/What/When/Where/ Why.
   - ➤ Answer "Why you" and "Why now" from the customer's perspective.
   - ➤ Distill 2–3 key messages and repeat them.

4. Deliver with presence; keep slides minimal
   - ➤ Be intentional about your state; practice until it's natural.
   - ➤ MVP slides only—visuals that help you tell the story, not walls of text.
   - ➤ Set the room and tech for success (space, AV, seating).

5. Listen consciously and handle objections as guidance
   - ➤ Stay open: full attention, non-judgment, empathy, patience.
   - ➤ Reflect back: "What I heard you say is . . . Did I get that right?"
   - ➤ Respond from presence (of mind/heart/body), not reactivity.

6. Analyze and iterate after presenting
   - ➤ Debrief quickly; gather team observations (energy shifts, body language).
   - ➤ Re-qualify gaps as needed and refine your offer/presentation.
   - ➤ Treat The Map as a living document throughout the cycle.

CHAPTER 13

Closing

This chapter may be brief, but its message is crucial.

If sealing the deal is not the smoothest part of the sales process, chances are you overlooked something earlier on between connecting and presenting. Now, you have the self-awareness, language, and precision of each step of the sales process to explore what and where you may have missed, a piece of the puzzle along the way.

Usually, I find that people stumble in the connecting and qualifying parts of the sales process. Or perhaps it was in the prospecting phase; your prospect wasn't the right person in the customer organization to catalyze the decision on your solution, or the customer didn't have sufficient funds and couldn't afford to buy from you.

I encourage you to work with others on your team, mentors, and leaders to explore what you may have missed. Don't do this in a vacuum. Be open, seek support, and explore your sales process with people you trust. I am always amazed at how much I learn when I include others in my discovery and often, I close the gap and the deal.

Sometimes, the close is ripe and all it takes is simply asking for the business. This step often requires courage, as requesting the final transaction can be daunting. The fear of rejection, a constant companion throughout the journey, can feel particularly intense in this moment.

Voicing your agreement to make it a reality might sound like this:

"Now that we've reviewed the paperwork, are all the details clear? Any lingering questions?"

"So, are you ready to proceed with signing?"

Closing means finalizing the contractual portion of the sales process. The contract outlines the product or service, often with legal jargon. Once signed, the agreed-upon exchange of goods or services for a set price within a specific timeframe is confirmed, kicking off the implementation (and/or delivery) phase.

I believe closing is the easiest part because if you've thoroughly qualified and presented, checking off all the boxes in the qualifying chapter, there should be no stone left unturned regarding the customer's needs and how your offering meets them. It's time to move ahead, formalize the commitment, and establish the timeline for funds to change hands. Some reps struggle with this, feeling uneasy about requesting the final transaction. My take is that they're likely anxious and may have missed something during qualifying. It's understandable to feel nervous, especially early in your career or with a high-stakes deal. If that's the case, I strongly advise seeking support from mentors and coaches. Don't be shy—get the help you need!

In summary, be meticulous in qualifying and presenting your sale. If you've listened and communicated consciously and made the customer feel heard, completing the transaction should unfold naturally as something they want. Be straightforward in your request and remain open and curious.

If the customer isn't quite ready to close but you've nurtured a strong connection and trust, they'll probably tell you what else needs to be qualified and addressed to reach the finish line.

What sets apart the best of the best is often hard to decipher. As a coach, I am an observer, leader, and student of masterful (sales) professionals, and the best way I can describe the best salespeople is a mélange of the following in no specific order: fierce, ambitious, rigorous, aware, lusting for knowledge and ideas, fiery desire to create powerful outcomes, all combined with a healthy tolerance for risk. What follows is a story of a sales professional who embodies all of these attributes.

Damien Madson: A Sales Success Story

Damien is a force of nature in the Central Florida commercial real estate scene. Every time I run into him, I'm struck by his vibrant energy and infectious smile. With over three decades of sales experience and impressive business results, he embodies the foundation of powerful salesmanship: creativity, resilience, courage, trustworthiness, strong relationships, and a genuine love for what he does.

His presence in a room is unmistakable. Respected in the community not just for his impressive track record, but for his unwavering positivity and steadfastness, Damien attacks each day with the same vigor and passion as when he first started out. And he does it because he loves it.

Damien's journey with sales started when he was a young door-to-door book salesman. He grew up with financial struggle and was ambitious. He wanted to make his way in the world. This fertile learning ground taught him how to connect quickly with people, handle objections and rejections, and maintain his enthusiasm through long, rigorous workdays. While others fizzled quickly, Damien thrived, laying the perfect foundation for the bigger, more elaborate real estate ventures of his future.

Fast-forward a couple of decades to a deal that

showcases Damien's expertise. Working with a large restaurant group on an 18-month project to consolidate over a dozen office buildings into one new, purpose-built facility, Damien faced a last-minute curveball at the close. The CEO announced that they wanted to move forward, but to own rather than lease a facility, which completely undermined the deal's premise. When he heard the announcement, Damien's gut dropped, but he didn't miss a beat. He knew his client well, understood their concerns and the criteria for the deal. He had a depth of knowledge of the market and decided to make a bold move. He quickly secured the only suitable property in the marketplace as an investment for his firm and within a month, sold it to the restaurant group, making a $3.5 million profit.

"This deal taught me so much," Damien reflected. "It showed me the importance of knowing the market inside and out, being able to pivot quickly, and always looking for opportunity, even when a deal seems to be falling apart. But most importantly, it reinforced my belief that in real estate, and in life, you've got to be willing to take calculated risks. If you believe in something, go for it. The rewards can be incredible."

Damien is a textbook example of a willingness to take calculated risks in a marketplace he understands. What sets him apart is his deep-seated passion that goes beyond the need for security or ego. It's an almost spiritual connection with his work. He shared a unique ritual he performs for new properties: "I go there by myself," he told me, his eyes lighting up. "And I meditate. People ask me what I'm doing, and I just say, 'I'm fine, just let me do my thing.' I believe in order to sell this property, you have to have a spiritual connection to it. So I'm creating that connection right now."

This spiritual approach extends to his entire career. "I'm very passionate about this," he explained. "It's not just a job, it is something I love." That love fuels his willingness to learn and to take risks, a quality he tries to instill in others. He often tells his interns and two sons, "Boys, take more risks in life. Do not hold back."

That's the essence of Damien's approach to sales and to life: Connect deeply. Know your stuff. Love what you do. Take risks. And when things get tough, keep moving forward. It's a philosophy that's not just about making money—it's about creating a rich, fulfilling career and life.

Damien's restaurant story beautifully illustrates the importance of requalifying when unexpected changes arise near closing. When Damien found himself facing a potential deal-breaker, instead of panicking or trying to force the original plan, he recognized this as a signal to requalify the client's needs. He quickly reassessed the situation, considering the new information about the client's preferences and the current market conditions. This requalification process allowed Damien to pivot swiftly, identifying a new solution that aligned with the client's updated requirements. By securing a suitable property and offering it for sale, he not only salvaged the deal but also significantly increased its value.

This scenario underscores the critical nature of remaining flexible and open to requalification throughout the sales process, even in its final stages. Damien's ability to listen, adapt, and creatively problem-solve in response to new information ultimately led to a successful close and a win-win outcome for all parties involved.

KEY TAKEAWAYS

1. Closing is the easiest step—if you've done the work
   - If connecting, qualifying, and presenting were thorough, closing should feel natural.
   - Stumbles at this stage usually signal something was missed earlier in the process.

2. Ask clearly and with courage
   - Simple questions work: "Are you ready to proceed?" or "Any details we need to clarify before signing?"
   - Courage is key—fear of rejection is normal, but directness builds trust.

3. Seek support when needed
   - Involve mentors, peers, and leaders if you feel stuck.
   - Don't close in a vacuum—fresh perspective often reveals gaps.

4. Formalize the commitment
   - Closing means finalizing the contract and confirming next steps.
   - Once signed, funds and timelines are locked in, and implementation begins.

5. Stay curious and open
   - If the customer hesitates, listen. They'll often tell you what's missing.
   - Use this feedback to loop back, requalify, or clarify as needed.

14

Implementing
& Follow-up

Implementing

The implementation phase of the sales process is typically handled by those tasked with delivering and operating your business once the agreement is signed. This is where the promise(s) made throughout the sales journey come to fruition, the exchange of goods and/or services takes place. This is the point of the sales process where the customer gets to experience the value and benefits of their investment. It is often the most tangible part of the sales process for them. It is crucial to do this well in order to produce the customer's satisfaction.

If you do it well, you can achieve a much higher likelihood of future sales and referrals, ultimately lowering the cost (money, energy, and time) required for future sales and of doing business.

I always made it a priority to stay closely connected with the customer and internal stakeholders in my organization who oversaw delivery and fulfillment. While I (like most sales reps) had to count on others to actually deliver the product or service outlined in the contract, I wanted to cultivate my relationship with the customer well beyond the closing stage to foster repeat business. So, I had my finger on the pulse of deliveries no matter what.

Implementation is all about honoring the contractual commitment. It also frequently triggers additional payments for the products or services provided, revenue recognition, and compensation for the sales professionals involved. In longer-term subscription or service agreements, this fulfillment continues for the duration of the contract, which can span several years.

When selling a product or service, I took responsibility for staying close to the implementation process—in my case, it was the logistics and training fulfillment teams. In many cases, successful sales professionals stay aware of (and even actively involved in) the implementation process. This makes sense. It is a high-risk time for the deal. If this part doesn't go according to plan, it can derail the deal and, in some instances, jeopardize the entire relationship.

Just as Jorge showed me the immense value of fostering genuine connections over time, he also helped me understand that my role wasn't finished just because the deal was inked. Keeping open lines of communication with both the customer and my internal team was crucial. I wanted to ensure that the trust and rapport I'd worked so hard to establish carried through seamlessly to the implementation phase.

If any hiccups or challenges arose during fulfillment, I aimed to be a bridge between the customer and our operations personnel. By maintaining that personal touch and accountability, I could help smooth out any wrinkles and keep the relationship on solid ground.

Ultimately, successful implementation is about more than just ticking boxes and going through the motions. It's a vital opportunity to reinforce your credibility, demonstrate your ongoing commitment, and lay the groundwork for future business. It is where you and the company you represent earn the trust that was granted by the customer at the close. When you stay engaged and invested in the customer's success beyond the sale itself, you're planting seeds that can bear fruit for years to come.

When you approach this crucial, often tangible stage with the same level of care and dedication you bring to the rest of the sales process, you'll be well on your way to forging lasting, mutually beneficial partnerships.

Follow-up

Once you have gotten through some, if not all, of the implementation, your next sales cycle will seamlessly begin as part of this final step of the sales process. As you follow up with your customer to maintain your connection, you'll discover what worked, what needs further support, and what is unfolding with your customer. If the implementation phase is well-handled, then in all likelihood, you'll have a satisfied customer, and future business will come at a much lower opportunity cost. After all, that's the intention of the entire sales process up to this point. As long as your customer is happy, they are unlikely to be swayed away from you for future business. The trust they have in you will likely be a barrier to entry for another competitor to overcome.

Having a certain cadence for follow-up is wise and depends on a multitude of variables in your market. It's important to know how often you need to reconnect with your customer and make this a conscious practice. Some (but not all) of the variables include the life cycle of your product or service and how quickly someone forgets who you are, which will surprise you no matter how satisfied they are with their purchase. If you lose touch, it's likely that it will be an opening for a competitor, so be prudent about this. Know that you are nurturing your future sales and stepping into the cycle of the sales process all over again by marketing yourself, showcasing the success of your already implemented deal, and reconnecting with your customer for the future, where they may likely be a prospect yet again in a future sale.

The goal of having a powerful sales process is that future business will be closed and implemented at a lower opportunity cost, with less time and energy required to achieve another deal.

Moving forward, it's vital to have a relevant reason to be present with your customer. Commit to being someone who is interesting, well-read, personable, open, and can create meaningful conversation. If you do all of this, the likelihood is that you will find a lot of success with ease and delight.

Remember, the sales process is a continuous cycle of nurturing relationships, delivering on promises, and consistently earning trust. By making a conscious effort to stay connected with your customers and being a reliable resource for them, you'll find that future opportunities arise naturally, with far less effort required on your part.

Ultimately, mastering the art of follow-up is about embodying the same qualities that make you a successful salesperson: attentiveness, reliability, and a genuine commitment to your customer's success. When you approach this crucial phase with the same level of dedication and care you bring to the rest of the sales process, you'll be well on your way to building a thriving, sustainable business built on a foundation of trust and mutual success.

As Jorge's wisdom has shown time and again, the key to long-term success in sales is to never lose sight of the human connection at the heart of every transaction. By staying engaged, demonstrating your value, and always putting your customer's needs first, you'll not only close more deals—you'll build the kind of relationships that will propel your career to new heights.

KEY TAKEAWAYS

1. Implementation delivers the promises you made
   - ➤ This is when the customer experiences the value of their investment.
   - ➤ A smooth implementation reinforces trust and credibility.
   - ➤ Poor execution here can jeopardize the relationship and future sales.

2. Stay engaged beyond the contract
   - ➤ Stay connected with both your internal delivery team and the customer.
   - ➤ Act as a bridge if challenges arise to maintain trust.
   - ➤ Your presence shows commitment and accountability.

3. Follow up with intention
   - ➤ Check in consistently to ensure satisfaction and uncover new needs.
   - ➤ A strong follow-up cadence lowers the cost and effort of future sales.
   - ➤ Staying present prevents competitors from taking your place.

4. Think of the sales process as a cycle
   - ➤ Successful implementation leads naturally into follow-up and future prospecting.
   - ➤ Each stage sets up the next, reducing time, energy, and risk for you and your customer.
   - ➤ Long-term success comes from nurturing trust and human connection beyond the deal.

CHAPTER 15

Your Journey Forward

Throughout this book, we've explored the fundamentals of exceptional sales performance—from the inner work of knowing yourself to the outer work of mastering your craft. We've examined the practices that create sustainable success, the frameworks that guide sound decisions, and the ways of being that enable authentic connection.

As we conclude, let's explore how these elements come together in moments of truth—when knowing yourself and knowing your craft merge, when you are put to the test and you choose wisely. The following story is a perfect illustration of how sales mastery transforms into leadership mastery.

Integrating Masterful Salesmanship into Conscious Leadership

At its core, leadership is a continuous series of sales conversations: You are always selling vision, confidence, and possibility—whether it is to customers, peers, your upper leadership team, or those who report to you. This work often calls for playful wisdom, even in the face of serious business challenges. One February afternoon, while en route to a meeting, Francois, a global head of sales received an urgent call about the regular Friday strategy circle meeting. This wasn't just any meeting—it included the company's power players: the CEO, CFO, heads of marketing, R&D, and production.

What many leaders discover too late is that selling isn't just about external customers—some of your most crucial sales happen within your own organization. Just as you need to read the room with clients, you must do the same with your leadership team. Sometimes even more skillfully, as these stakeholders know all your plays and patterns.

As Francois listened to the CFO's voice on the call, something caught his attention. The CFO was known throughout the organization for his steady, calming presence—a stabilizing force in even the most turbulent times. But today, there was an unusual edge in his typically measured tone. Years of working together had attuned Francois to these subtle shifts in energy and temperament. Despite being on his way to an important customer meeting, his intuition told him his presence was needed at this internal gathering. The numbers were behind target, and he could sense the anxiety building among the leadership team.

This moment of clarity didn't come by accident. It was the result of years of deliberate practice—countless meetings, failures, successes, and most importantly, the inner work of developing self-awareness and business acumen. Like an athlete who has put in thousands of repetitions, he had invested the time to know both himself and his craft deeply enough that he could trust his instincts when they spoke.

Without hesitation, he called the customer to reschedule and turned his car around. What happened next wasn't planned—it emerged from a wealth of experience and deep self-knowledge. Walking into the tension-filled room, he made an unexpected move:

he bet the CFO an expensive case of red wine that they would hit their sales targets for the year.

This wasn't just a bet—it was a masterful transformation of energy, a perfect example of selling confidence to your own leadership team. In that moment, what had been a pressure-cooker of stress became something different. The simple act of making it playful, while backing it with authentic confidence, changed the entire dynamic. The other leaders in the room could feel it. They didn't just hear his words; they sensed his embodied knowing that the team would deliver.

This kind of leadership presence comes from a paradoxical combination of rigorous preparation and complete surrender. You must put in the work—the long hours of learning, the careful attention to detail, the cultivation of business insight—but then you must also learn to let go. It's only when you've built such a deep reservoir of experience and self-awareness that you can trust yourself to release control and allow your wisdom to emerge naturally in crucial moments.

And yes, the team performed well that year. Francois won the bet, received the case of wine, though that was hardly the point. The real victory was in recognizing when to step in and how to transform anxiety into possibility, not through complex strategies or stern declarations, but through authentic confidence and a touch of playfulness. It was a moment where deep self-knowledge met business acumen, creating something more powerful than either one could achieve alone—a masterclass in shifting and creating connection and possibility.

Some Final Words

Let's reflect on the journey we've shared. What began as a framework for sales has revealed itself to be much more—a pathway to self-discovery, authentic connection, and sustainable success in both business and life.

You now possess two powerful sets of intelligence: a deeper understanding of yourself and a refined grasp of the sales process. This dual knowledge is your competitive advantage. Understanding your triggers, patterns, and ways of being allows you to show up more authentically and effectively in every interaction. Meanwhile, your enhanced comprehension of each step in the sales process—from marketing through following up—gives you a roadmap for converting opportunities into results.

The magic happens when these two forms of intelligence work in harmony. When you are fully present and aware of yourself while systematically working through the sales process, you create what I call "conscious momentum." This is where deals start flowing more naturally, relationships deepen organically, and success becomes more sustainable.

But here's a critical point that I can't emphasize enough—your most valuable asset in sales isn't your product knowledge or your network; it's you. Just as a professional athlete must maintain peak physical condition to perform at their best, you must take care of your mind, body, and heart to sustain excellence in sales.

Remember the discussion about creating conditions for success? This means:

➤ Getting adequate sleep (7–8 hours)

➤ Maintaining regular exercise

➤ Eating nutritious food

➤ Practicing meditation or mindfulness

➤ Making time for play and joy

➤ Nurturing relationships outside of work

These aren't luxury items or "nice-to-haves." They are essential foundations for sustainable success. I learned this lesson the hard way through my neck injury, and I hope you can learn it the easier way through these pages.

As you implement the practices in this book—and I say this as someone who's been called "the tornado"—you must grant yourself the time and space to do so effectively. Rome wasn't built in a day, and neither is sales mastery. Take time to:

➤ Review your current opportunity pipeline through this new lens.

➤ Practice the breathing exercises before important meetings.

➤ Work through The Map for each key prospect.

➤ Craft and refine your introductions.

➤ Design presentations with intention and story.

➤ Build in reflection time after each significant interaction.

Remember Jorge's patient relationship-building, Thomas's persistent trust-building with Bill, and Damien's spiritual connection to his properties. These weren't overnight successes; they were the result of consistent, conscious effort over time.

As you move forward, treat this process as an ongoing journey rather than a destination. Some days you'll embody these principles beautifully; other days you'll fall back into old patterns. That's perfectly normal. The key is to keep returning to these practices, refining your approach, and trusting in the process.

What becomes clear through experiences like these is that as you integrate deeper knowledge of yourself and your craft, you become more capable, more trusted, more powerful, and your results speak for themselves. For exceptional salespeople, this mastery often reveals new paths. You may find, like Francois, that leadership becomes a natural evolution. Or you may choose to deepen your individual excellence, achieving remarkable results with greater ease and flow. Whatever path you choose, the power that comes from this integration isn't about control or dominance; it's about creating space for you and others to succeed, transforming energy when needed, and holding steady in uncertain times. While the journey from sales excellence to conscious leadership is a story for another book, the foundations we've built here will serve you well in any role in which you choose to grow.

I encourage you to start small. Pick one or two concepts that resonated most strongly and begin implementing them immediately. Perhaps it's the BE. DO. HAVE. framework, or maybe it's The Map for qualifying prospects. Whatever speaks to you, start there and build momentum.

You have everything you need to create extraordinary results in your sales career. The principles and practices in this book aren't just theoretical—they're battle-tested strategies that have helped countless professionals transform their approach to sales and achieve remarkable outcomes.

Trust yourself. Trust the process. And most importantly, enjoy the journey. After all, as we've learned, the best results often come when we are operating from a place of authentic engagement rather than forced effort.

Here's to your success—not just in closing deals, but in creating meaningful connections and lasting impact in your work and life, while maintaining your own well-being along the way.

Now, take a deep breath, open your calendar, and block some time to plan your next steps. Your future self will thank you for it.

afterword

Congratulations! You have just made a significant investment in your career. This book is a treasure trove of practices, tools, and frameworks that truly work. I have spent my entire career in sales and sales leadership. Over the last several years, I've held the most intense sales role of all as a CEO of a large healthcare group. While I've lived alongside Ilana while she developed and refined the framework in this book, I have also been able to implement many of these concepts into my organization. When you fully engage with both Part 1 and Part 2, you will see tremendous results.

It can be tempting (especially for those of us who are driven by results) to skip the "emotional stuff" and jump straight into the mechanics of prospecting, presenting, and closing. After all, the tangible tactics of Part 2 may feel more practical, more urgent, or more comfortable to measure. But if you gloss over Part 1, you'll be missing the foundation on which all those tactics depend. Part 1 is where you become FIERCE. The more in-tune you are with your own inner-state, the better you can listen, learn from, and respond to your customer's true needs and desires.

If you ever find yourself struggling to get traction with the strategies in Part 2, chances are the gap isn't in your technique, it's in the inner work of Part 1. Sales is not only about what you say or do; it's about who you are being in the moment you say it. Without presence, intention, and authenticity, even the best-crafted pitch falls flat.

I've watched Ilana teach this work to executives, seasoned sales leaders, and people just starting out. Every time, the breakthrough comes when someone slows down long enough to do the deeper work—when they stop trying to "fix" their sales process and instead strengthen themselves. From that place, the tactics of Part 2 stop feeling like effort and start flowing with ease.

If you hold a "C" level title, are a VP, Director, or people manager in any way shape or form, this book is a powerful tool for you too. Any people manager or department head is ultimately a salesperson. You are selling a vision, an idea, or even a corporate culture daily. Use this book (especially Part 1) to develop and hone a new set of leadership skills. The more fully you invest in developing yourself—your presence, your awareness, your way of being—the more powerful and effortless your results will be.

Now, the choice is yours. You can set this book down and return to business as usual, or you can lean in, revisit the hard questions, and do the work that will separate you from the average. If you commit to both the inner game and the outer process, you will discover what it truly means to be FIERCE.

—Brent Williams

acknowledgments

This book would not exist without the people who have walked alongside me, challenged me, and believed in me through the seasons of my career and my life. I am deeply grateful to each of you.

First, to Jorge, who embodied the joy, class, and mastery of sales from the very first day I met him. Your generosity, humor, and ability to make everyone feel seen planted the earliest seeds of what became this framework. You showed me that sales is about more than closing deals—it's about authentic human connection and the joy of creation.

To Lucas, whose invitation to co-facilitate my very first workshop changed the trajectory of my career. Thank you for trusting me and for giving me the opportunity to step into leadership in a way that continues to ripple through this work.

To Thomas, whose trustworthiness, heart, curiosity, and rigor have always stood out to me. You taught me that the toughest customers often become the most valuable relationships when we show up consistently, listen deeply, and hold our ground with respect. Thank you for being so smart, capable, reliable, and supportive—and for believing in me as much as you do.

I am grateful for colleagues, clients, and friends who reminded me that sales is both an art and a craft: Jeff, for modeling tremendous courage and the value of connection; Damien, for your steady wisdom; Michael, for demonstrating that resilience and honesty under pressure are the greatest sales strategies; Kaitlin, for your openness, clarity, and willingness to shift relationships at key moments; and Francois, whose leadership, unwavering belief, and trust gave me permission to spread my wings, take bold steps, and claim my place in this work. Each of you shaped this book in ways both direct and subtle, and I am honored to call you colleagues and friends. To my teams at Siemens: Jeff J, Ana, Katie, Rich, Craig, Doug, Troy, Bill C, Nanci, Blake, Bob, Sara, April, Matt M, Dave D, David G, Andy, Gonzo, Gustavo, Judy, Raj, Roy, Wayne, Chuck, Steve; to my customers: Beth, Andrea, Rochelle, Kim, Liz, Mike G, Fran, Denise, Suzanne, Lorenzo, Abel, Bill K, Dr. Ziffer, Dr. Hannah, and so many more who were key actors in my professional life, who filled my world with laughter, challenge, success, cool conversations, deep connection, and friendship—thank you.

To the countless teachers and thinkers who have shaped me over the last two decades—both those whose wisdom fills these pages and those whose names do not appear here—thank you. With deep gratitude to Rick Rubin, Gay Hendricks, Jim Dethmer and the Conscious Leadership Group, Phil Stutz, and Viktor Frankl.

To my dearest friends: It took me four decades to find such friendships, and it was worth the wait. Thank you for making me laugh, for nurturing, challenging, and supporting me. Thank you for being exactly the way you are and exactly the way you aren't—for being my partners in adventure and discovery. Ron, Bradley, Andrew, Anna, Rune, Jay, Nicole, Kate, Clay, Larry.

To Dr. Gentzy Franz, my collaborator and friend. Your keen precision with words and clarity of thought bring extraordinary insight to every exchange we share. Thank you not only for gifting this book with the Foreword and the elegant design of the Stimulus–Presence–Wandering diagram, but also for co-creating new content with me and for sharpening and challenging my thinking.

To my mother, who called me the "tornado" and taught me the power of speed, intensity, and resilience. To my genius father, who showed me what diligence and precision look like, and how discipline in any subject (his was math) can foster mastery. To my sister, a second mom to me—thank you for always encouraging me to be unabashedly the way I am.

To my dearest husband, Brent, whose extraordinary business acumen, encouragement, love, tenderness, and support catalyzed my transition into my second career and without whom I would not be the woman I am today. You have surprised me again and again with what is possible in partnership—showing me a depth of love, respect, and devotion I didn't know enough to dream of when I was younger. Thank you for your mind, heart, body, and soul.

Finally, to my audacious, inspiring daughters, Orli and Ayla. You have been both my grounding and my inspiration. Thank you for being such exquisite humans and for teaching me what I need to learn. I love you and am incredibly proud of you.

To all the salespeople out there, this book is as much yours as it is mine. May it serve as a testament to the power of mentorship, courage, and love in the pursuit of mastery.

about the author

Ilana Williams is an executive coach, leadership consultant, and strategist who helps leaders
and organizations unlock performance through
conscious leadership, authentic connection,
and courageous growth. Earlier in her career at
Siemens, she turned a challenger product into
the market leader in her territory, outpacing

competitors who had long dominated the space. That experience
shaped her understanding of trust, influence, and human behavior
in high-stakes environments. She is the founder of **Elan Consulting
Firm**, where she partners with executives, teams, and entrepreneurs
to navigate growth with clarity and intention. Ilana lives in Florida
with her husband, Brent, and her daughters, Orli and Ayla.

www.ingramcontent.com/pod-product-compliance
Lightning Source LLC
Chambersburg PA
CBHW060427130626
46555CB00005B/2243

* 9 7 9 8 9 9 3 3 6 3 7 1 4 *